NIETZSCHE

THE ANTICHRIST & THE ANTIPOLITICAL

Dionysus, Mythology, & Aristocratic Radicalism

GWENDOLYN TAUNTON

Nietzsche: The Antichrist & the Antipolitical
Dionysus, Mythology, & Aristocratic Radicalism
Gwendolyn Taunton

Thema Classification:
QRAB (Philosophy of Religion), QDTS (Social & Political Philosophy), QRSG (Ancient Greek Mythology), QDHR (Western Philosophy).
978-0-6487660-6-3
MANTICORE PRESS
www.manticore.press

Of all that is written, I love only what a person hath written with his blood. Write with blood, and thou wilt find that blood is spirit.

It is no easy task to understand unfamiliar blood; I hate the reading idlers.

- Friedrich Nietzsche, *Thus Spake Zarathustra*

CONTENTS

PROLEGOMENON

ON READERS AND WRITERS

Friedrich Nietzsche is undoubtedly one of the most famous philosophers. He has exerted enormous posthumous influence on the arts, politics, and even the occult realm. Moreover, this influence has not waned in the contemporary era. Yet, despite his popularity, Nietzsche is still widely misunderstood. To understand Nietzsche one must read his writing in the spirit in which it was composed. Many readers lightly peruse his works, pause to ruminate over a few remarks, and then cease to read any further. This has led to numerous misconceptions regarding Nietzsche's core concepts. For one to understand Nietzsche's writing, it must be read in full and in the context of the cultural environment with which he was contemporaneous. Statements that appear contradictory are not when framed in the correct narrative, but Nietzsche often strives to render this problematic for the reader by encapsulating concepts in a minefield of explosive metaphors, symbols, and cryptic riddles. Nietzsche enjoys baiting readers with dangerously ambiguous statements, which like an irate sphinx, may suddenly pounce upon any potential Oedipus who fails to respond correctly. This intentional ambiguity is a major obstacle for newcomers to his work.

In this regard, the level of complexity cunningly crafted by Nietzsche is deliberate, for he was not writing for the average reader – to do so would have been abhorrent to him. In *Thus Spake Zarathustra* (Of Reading and Writing), Nietzsche refers to 'idle readers' and

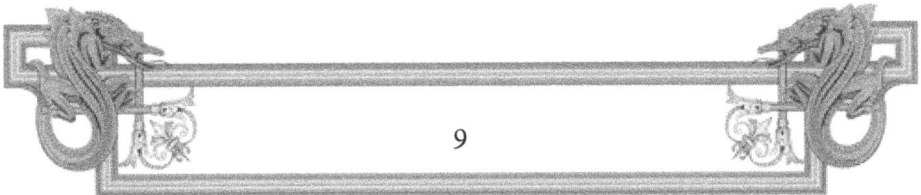

their inability to understand the essential *spirit* with which an author writes – and this is why these idle readers are doomed to misunderstand not just Nietzsche, but any literary work. Nietzsche's 'spirit', in particular, is obfuscated from all but the most astute of audiences. In fact, Nietzsche's preferred audience is an extremely small one, and it is to these chosen few that he addressed his real ideas. For this reason, many people reject Nietzsche's writing because they find it incomprehensible or claim that his work is inconsistent. To comprehend Nietzsche's literary style correctly requires an *active* reader endowed with the ability to *translate the spirit* of his works.

The two most widely misconstrued aspects of Nietzsche's philosophy are his views on religion and politics. Concerning religion, his philosophy is severely truncated to 'God is dead', without bothering to delve deeper into the phrase's contextual setting or examining his use of terms borrowed from ancient Greek mythology. The other problem stems from the various colorful interpretations of Nietzsche's political statements, which are often more reflections of the reader's own confirmation bias than they are of Nietzsche's actual opinion. Moreover, this issue encompasses the entire political spectrum. This is amply illustrated by the fact that some authors fallaciously associate Nietzsche with a diverse range of ideologies, including nationalism, anarchism, and liberalism. The copious range of spiritual protagonists is also extremely varied. Therefore, *Nietzsche: The Antichrist & the Antipolitical* intends to explain the finer points of Nietzsche's opinions on religion, culture, and politics.

The first section of the book will explore the specific significance of Nietzsche's famous Apollo and Dionysus dyad. This will demonstrate how Nietzsche was influenced by other authors in Germany and utilized sources on ancient Greek traditions. It will then explain how Dionysus' use as an allegorical figure is integral to Nietzsche's theories on religion – including the widely misunderstood 'Death of

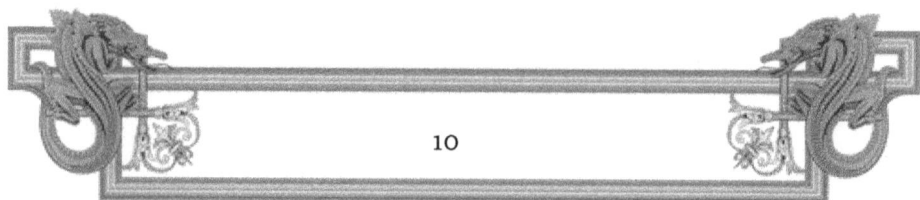

God' and Nietzsche's seemingly incongruous comments about the Antichrist.

The second half of the book concentrates on political and cultural issues. Nietzsche's views on religion are integral to understanding this and his antipolitical philosophy. Only by fully comprehending his perspective can one even begin to explore the political dimension, which lies so far outside of the mainstream that it is challenging for many readers. His real political system is a new one, which does not exist, nor has it existed at any point in human history. It is both radical and unique. To a certain extent, Nietzsche is what Walter Kaufmann once described as an "antipolitical individual who seeks self-perfection far from the modern world."[1] However, this *antipolitical individualism* is far more radical than merely abstaining from politics and being an individualist. Nietzsche's antipolitical stance is part of his broader cultural agenda, which Georg Brandes named *aristocratic radicalism*. This is not traditional aristocracy, rather as the name implies, it is an altogether different beast.

Nietzsche: The Antichrist & the Antipolitical strives to present Nietzsche's authentic ideas on religion and politics from an unbiased stance. As such, the intent is to convey Nietzsche's ideas neutrally, without an attempt to promote any religions or political platforms. The book has not been composed to conform with existing ideologies, nor to enhance or detract from any spiritual beliefs, but rather to present the more controversial aspects of Nietzsche's philosophy as he intended them to be – ideas designed for the few and unpalatable for many. It will not be a sugar-coated placebo, and it may be a bitter pill for some to swallow.

It is a book for the active reader who can examine an idea independently, whether they agree or disagree.

---

[1] DOMBOWSKY, D., *Nietzsche's Machiavellian Politics* (New York: Palgrave MacMillan, 2004), 69.

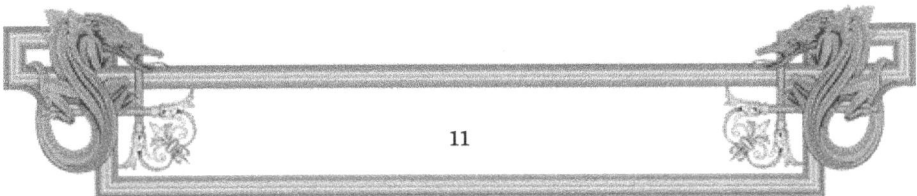

CHRISTIANITY, DIONYSUS, & THE ANTICHRIST

ON MYTHOLOGY & RELIGION

The Resurrection of Dionysus

The Birth of Tragedy was my first revaluation of all values: with that, I again plant myself in the soil out of which I draw all that I will and can – *I, the last disciple of the philosopher Dionysus – I, the teacher of the eternal recurrence.*

- Friedrich Nietzsche

Friedrich Nietzsche is well-known for his proclamation that "God is dead," but can an immortal idea ever truly perish? Or does it merely change form, recreating itself anew in every epoch or cultural milieu? Dionysus, Nietzsche's favorite mythological figure, is undoubtedly one that can be reborn, just as Christ is also believed to have risen from the dead. This is not the real crux of the issue, however. What is implicit in Nietzsche's conception of Dionysus is the problem of whether or not religion and mythology can also undergo a rebirth and that resurrection itself can be a form of eternal recurrence.

Most of Nietzsche's early writings revolve around postulating a duality consisting of the two Hellenic deities Apollo and Dionysus. What is less apparent, however, is the complicated relationship Nietzsche creates between mythology, religion, and culture. To fully understand how this impacts on his theories of culture, society, and politics, it is imperative to first understand his views on religion and mythology. All of the elements of Nietzsche's philosophy need to be examined in conjunction to visualize the complete picture. When considered in isolation, they appear contradictory to some readers.

In Nietzsche's view, the characteristics of the god Apollo are reflected and absorbed by his polar opposite, Dionysus. He first describes this relationship as early as *The Birth of Tragedy*, his first major work, in which he elaborates the theory that there are two different forces entwined in human nature – the Apollonian and the Dionysian – and subsequently modifies it in his later works. Though this topic has been examined frequently by philosophers, it has not been sufficiently explained in terms of its relation to the Greek myths concerning the two gods in question. Religion, for Nietzsche, has both its beginning and end in Hellenic mythology.

Unsurprisingly, the Hellenic tradition was one of Nietzsche's areas of academic focus. Nietzsche's interest in this line of research is illustrated by his exploration of the use of mythology as a tool to shape culture. *The Birth of Tragedy* draws heavily from Greek myth and literature, and also lays out much of the groundwork upon which he would develop his later premises. Setting the tone at the very beginning of *The Birth of Tragedy*, Nietzsche writes:

> We shall have gained much for the science of aesthetics, once we perceive not merely by logical inference, but with the immediate certainty of vision, that the continuous development of art is bound up with the *Apollonian* and *Dionysian* duality – just as procreation depends on the duality of the sexes, involving perpetual strife with only periodically intervening reconciliations. The terms Dionysian and Apollonian we borrow from the Greeks, who disclose to the discerning mind the profound mysteries of their view of art, not, to be sure, in

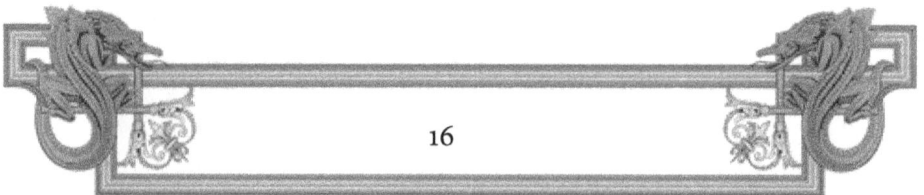

concepts, but in the intensely clear figures of their gods. Through Apollo and Dionysus, the two art deities of the Greeks, we come to recognize that in the Greek world, there existed a tremendous opposition.[1]

Several of Nietzsche's ideas are built upon this initial foundation and ultimately derived from a Hellenic perspective. However, this was not a unique concept, and Nietzsche's views did not develop in isolation. These concepts evolved from earlier, pre-existing sources which were very much in vogue in the German academic circles of his era. Greek history was a prestigious area of research, referred to collectively as Germanic Philhellenism. It was a form of cultural revival in which Germans looked back to ancient Greece for sources of inspiration to reinvigorate their own culture.

Alterthumswissenschaft was also a popular academic discipline in Germany because it was not "overtly political along the lines of 'nation' and 'religion' and was able to provide a utopian intertwining of Germany and Greece."[2] At the time, ancient Greece was revered as the pinnacle of European heritage, and the Germans began emulating certain aspects of it. Vassilis Lambropoulos writes that these new "educated Germans saw themselves as the modern Greeks, the inheritors of ancient culture."[3] As a consequence of this Hellenic revival, many theories began to emerge which were not inherently religious, but that drew strong parallels with the Hellenic Tradition and its religion and civilization.

---

[1] PORTER, J. I., *The Invention of Dionysus: An Essay on the Birth of Tragedy* (Stanford, CA: Stanford University Press, 2002), 40.

[2] EMDEN, C. J., *Friedrich Nietzsche and the Politics of History* (Cambridge: Cambridge University Press, 2010), 27.

[3] BAMBACH, C., "The Idea of the Archaic in German Thought: Creuzer, Bachofen, Nietzsche, Heidegger" in *The Archaic: The Past in the Present*, ed. BISHOP, P. (New York: Routledge, 2012), 149.

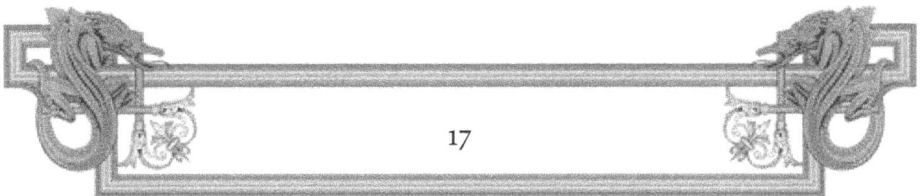

This era of Germanic Philhellenism began with the works of J. J. Winckelmann, who claimed that the path to Germanic greatness lay in "imitating the ancients [...] the Greeks in particular, and the generation of German thinkers reconstitutes its image of German identity and its possibilities."[4] Winckelmann's depiction of Hellenic Greece was therefore not only an academic work but also a cultural one, providing "a powerful counter-image to the political and cultural particularism of the German states in the earlier nineteenth century and beyond."[5] In contrast to Nietzsche, Winckelmann's new Germanic 'Greece' was based on a sedate, peaceful, and classical society. This view remained dominant in academic circles until it was challenged by the release of Friedrich Creuzer's *Symbolik und Mythologie der alten Volker, besonders der Greichen* (*Symbolism and Mythology of the Ancients, Especially the Greeks*). This book offered a very different depiction of ancient Greece that uncovered a hidden history of "bloody sacrifices, intoxicating orgies, primitive hunting rites and other liturgies that burst asunder Winckelmann's dreams."[6] Creuzer described a fundamental opposition in the Hellenic Tradition between the later Olympian gods of Homer and the earlier Chthonic deities connected to the Earth and the Underworld.[7] In contrast to Winckelmann's Apollo, the dark god Dionysus entered Germanic philosophy, becoming "the *Weltseele*, the Demiurge who was the creation of the material world and became intertwined with its suffering."[8]

Creuzer also inspired Johann Jakob Bachofen to write *Versuch uber die Grabersymbolik der Alten* (*Essay on the Symbolism of Ancient*

---

[4] Ibid., 148.

[5] EMDEN, *Friedrich Nietzsche and the Politics of History*, 27.

[6] BAMBACH, "The Idea of the Archaic in German Thought," 150.

[7] Ibid.

[8] Ibid., 151.

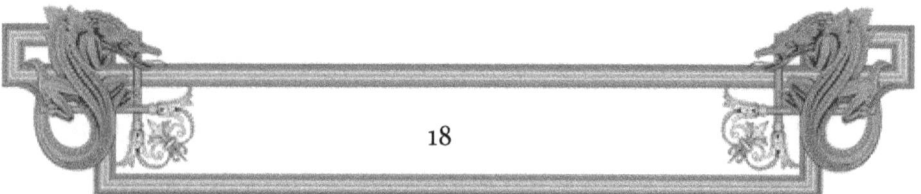

Tombs), *Das Mutterrecht* (*The Mother Right*), and *Die Sage von Tanaquil* (*The Saga of Tanaquil*). Bachofen reworked Creuzer's idea and established an opposition between earth-based, feminine forces (Telluric) and the masculine, sky-based forces (Uranic), which is an obvious parallel to Creuzer's original paradigm of Chthonic and Olympian deities.[9]

Before *The Birth of Tragedy's* composition, Nietzsche had encountered the works of both Bachofen[10] and Creuzer. Despite reading Creuzer, however, Nietzsche only referenced him once in his written works, during his early Basel lectures (1870—71).[11] Bachofen's influence on Nietzsche is tremendously apparent. The opposition Bachofen cites between Apollo and Demeter is analogous to Nietzsche's own Apollo/Dionysus pairing. Changing Demeter to Dionysus was a deliberate correction on Nietzsche's part because Hellenic imagery from Delphi depicts Apollo and Dionysus as being worshiped in tandem. Thus, for Nietzsche, Bachofen's opposition of the Sun/Sky/Male to the Lunar/Earth/Female erects a false dichotomy. The Uranic/Chthonic pairing was more complex, and it occurred between two male gods connected with the processes of higher cognition and creative vitality.

Moreover, Nietzsche's preference is for the darker, chthonic component of the dyad – Dionysus – which is considered to be inferior in the Uranic model espoused by Bachofen. Bachofen associated Dionysus with virile male sexuality connected to the Earth, and thus with the first (Tellurian) and the second (which Bachofen designates as matriarchal) stages of existence, because

---

[9] Ibid.

[10] Bachofen was a respected academic of the time, but his theories on ancient matriarchy have since been universally discredited.

[11] YELLE, R. A., "The Rebirth of Myth? Nietzsche's Eternal Recurrence and its Romantic Antecedents," in *NUMEN*, vol. 47, 184.

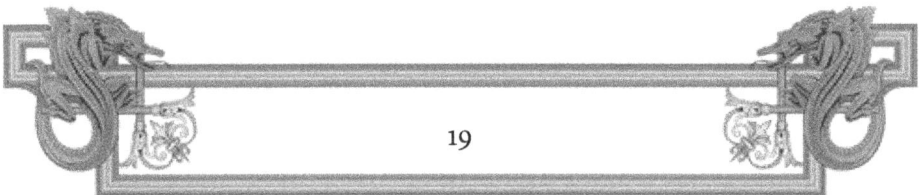

he believes Dionysus is connected to Demeter. Whilst Dionysus is associated with the Earth and fertility, he is also associated with the arts, the sun, and death. Demeter is more closely associated with agriculture and the Earth, while Dionysus' symbolic function is more abstract and complex. Demeter's purview is also more appropriately fertile land (Telluric), while Dionysus represents the aspect below the Earth (Chthonic). Although both refer to the ground, one refers to the tangible firmament of the soil and the other to an intangible domain located beneath the surface.

Aside from the issue of erroneously portraying Dionysus primarily as a horticultural deity, the logic of arbitrarily assigning the god to a feminine role is also dubious. While Dionysus is sometimes depicted as a hermaphrodite, he is also associated with phallic symbolism. Apollo, on the other hand, is not purely a heterosexual deity and has a high proportion of male lovers. There is therefore no clear-cut case for assigning either of them to a fixed gender dyad that corresponds to 'masculine vs. feminine' gender preferences. Moreover, there are broader issues involved with ascribing male and female sexuality to the two gods. Firstly, if gods existed, they would be beyond human form, and it is extremely reductionist to attempt to inscribe mortal biology upon an incorporeal force or deity. Secondly, it is a very human tendency to seek patterns in nature that are not actually present. This need to quantify patterns leads to faulty reasoning. To diminish gods, nature, and civilization down to a rigid polarity based on human sexuality is not only absurdly anthropocentric, it is also extraordinarily reductionist and strips everything of its complexity, rendering them as nothing more than a remarkably simplistic 'black and white' view of the world. Nietzsche's transposition of Dionysus for Apollo had a different motivation, which will be explained in another chapter.

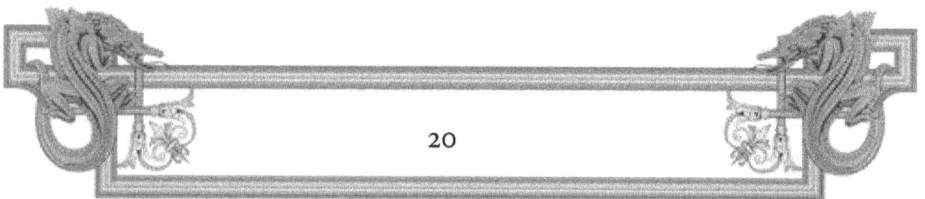

By correcting these perceived imperfections, Nietzsche came to be this lineage of German Philhellenism's most well-known representative, having surpassed and excelled both his predecessors Winckelmann and Bachofen, for as Max Baeumer remarks:

> The tradition of Dionysus and the Dionysian in German literature from Hamann and Herder to Nietzsche – as it has been set forth for the first time from aesthetic manifestoes, from literary works, and from what today are obscure works of natural philosophy and mythology – bears eloquent witness to the natural-mystical and ecstatic stance of German Romanticists which reached its final culmination in the works of Friedrich Nietzsche.[12]

It was Nietzsche who fully established the tension and dialectic between Dionysus Zagreus of the "wild *dithyrambos* [...] full of labyrinths" and "the god of light Phoebus Apollo, the disciplined, well-ordered *paean*."[13] This is laid out in *The Birth of Tragedy*, where Nietzsche directs his critique against Philhellenic classicism and "Winckelmann's dream of Apollonian purity" by recreating a different vision of ancient Greece – one that is archaic, rather than classical.[14] Its repercussions would later be echoed by Walter F. Otto, Martin Heidegger, in the world of politics (Alfred Baeumler), by thinkers in the Weimar Republic, and by many others.

Besides the Greeks, Nietzsche was also profoundly influenced by Schopenhauer. It is only by studying Schopenhauer that the intricate nature of Nietzsche's *Will to Power* and its relationship to Dionysus can be fully understood. Schopenhauer believed that dealing with

---

[12] VON STUCKRAD, K., "Utopian Landscapes and Ecstatic Journeys: Friedrich Nietzsche, Hermann Hesse, and Mircea Eliade on the Terror of Modernity" in *NUMEN*, vol. 57, 80.

[13] BAMBACH, "The Idea of the Archaic in German Thought," 151.

[14] Ibid., 149.

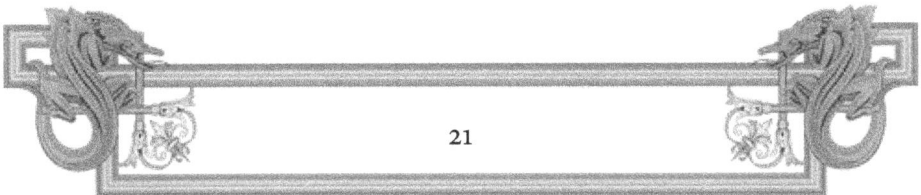

death was the first, and most essential, function of any authentic religious tradition.[15] The Dionysian element present in Nietzsche's writing is partially a "response to the Schopenhauerian philosophy of redemption."[16] According to Schopenhauer, both Judaism and Graeco-Roman paganism were failed religions because they lacked a properly developed doctrine of immortality.[17] Nietzsche sought to solve this problem by proving that the Hellenic Tradition did provide such a doctrine, for Dionysus, like Christ, is a 'dying god': he dies but is reborn through sacrifice.

Schopenhauer's *The World as Will and Representation* exerted an enormous influence on Nietzsche, but Nietzsche believed that the Will is positive, and he associated it with the Dionysian element. Dionysus is used as a symbol for both Will and Representation, which, according to Sokel, is "where Dionysus symbolizes the unconscious and the Will to Power, manifests as a dynamic energy, in eternal flux and change, the Heraclitean *panta rei*."[18] The Will is, therefore, a fathomless reservoir of vital primordial power. Since Dionysus is Chthonic, Nietzsche also believes the Will is likewise located below the surface of the mind and is thus associated with the subconscious. In *The Gay Science* Nietzsche openly acknowledges the power inherent within the subconscious:

> For the longest time, thinking was considered as only conscious, only now do we discover the truth that the greatest part of our intellectual activity lies in the unconscious [...] The unconscious

---

[15]   YOUNG, J., *Nietzsche and the Philosophy of Religion* (Cambridge: Cambridge University Press, 2006), 12.

[16]   SADLER, T., *Nietzsche: Truth and Redemption, Critique of the Postmodernist Nietzsche* (London: The Athlone Press, 1995), 129.

[17]   YOUNG, J., *Nietzsche and the Philosophy of Religion*, 12.

[18]   SOKEL, W., "On the Dionysian in Nietzsche: Monism and its Consequence" in *New Literary History*, vol. 36, no. 4.

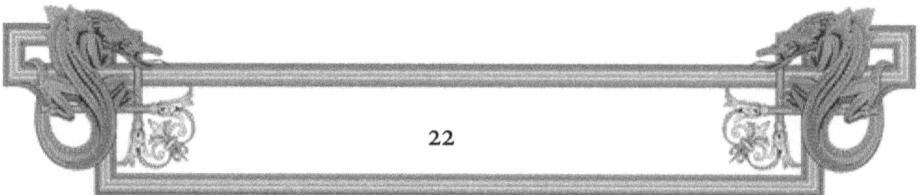

becomes a source of wisdom and knowledge that can reach into the fundamental aspects of human existence, while the intellect is held to be an abstracting and falsifying mechanism that is directed not toward truth but toward "mastery and possession."[19]

Nietzsche also makes other alterations to the earlier Apollo/ Dionysus dyad, and as Apollo gradually fades into insignificance altogether, his figure appears to have been superseded by Dionysus. Despite Apollo's conspicuous absence, he is still present, since any apparent opposition betwixt them is illusory, with the pairing echoing a mutual symbiosis or even a relationship based on commensalism. Thus, Apollo is still present, encapsulated within Nietzsche's transposition of Dionysus. What begins as a dichotomy in *The Birth of Tragedy* transforms into a synthesis in Nietzsche's later works, with the name Dionysus referring to the unified aspect of both Apollo *and* Dionysus, in what Nietzsche perceives to be their ultimate manifestation. This union is, according to Nietzsche, symbolized in art, and especially in Greek tragedy.[20] Greek tragedy portrays the union of the Apollonian and Dionysian as "a union in which Dionysian passion and dithyrambic madness merge with Apollonian measure and lucidity, and original chaos and pessimism are overcome in a tragic attitude that is affirmative and heroic."[21] What Nietzsche describes is the syncretism of Apollo and Dionysus in equal quantity, wherein "[t]he two art drives must unfold their powers in a strict proportion, according to the law of eternal justice."[22]

[19] PFEFFER, R., *Nietzsche: Disciple of Dionysus* (Lewisburg: Bucknell University Press, 1972), 113.

[20] Ibid., 31.

[21] Ibid., 51.

[22] PORTER, *The Invention of Dionysus*, 82.

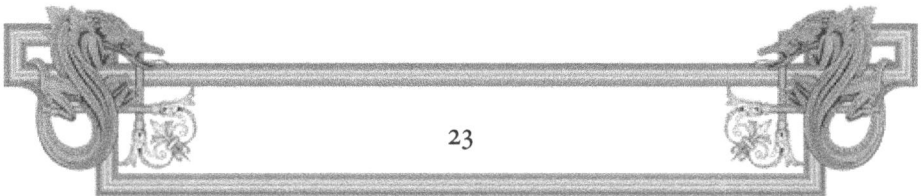

To attain ultimate mastery over the creative process, one must harness the impulses represented by both Apollo and Dionysus – the instinctual urge and raw creative power of Dionysus, coupled with the potent skill of Apollo's craftsmanship; or, more precisely, the subconscious creative power of the Will coupled with learned abilities. This infers that, for Nietzsche at least, art is a manifestation of the Will to Power, or art becoming *"die Gestaltung des Seienden in Ganzen."*[23] This concept of the artist as a creator, and of the creative process portrayed as a manifestation of the Will, is a core component of Nietzsche's thought; it is the artist, the creator who diligently scribes the new value tables. Nietzsche, therefore, announces a new form of artist who prefers to diligently craft human society by philosophizing, shaping the world with a sculptor's hammer.[24] Nietzsche also refers to this artist as the *Übermensch*. It the *Übermensch* – the artist as a leader – who demonstrates the unification and perfection of the Dionysian and the Apollonian as the manifestation of the Will.[25]

---

[23] Ibid., 205-206.

[24] The concept of 'philosophy with a hammer,' contrary to popular belief, refers to the art of sculpture, and does not imply the 'use of a hammer' in a violent or aggressive manner during philosophical debate.

[25] PFEFFER, R., *Nietzsche*, 114.

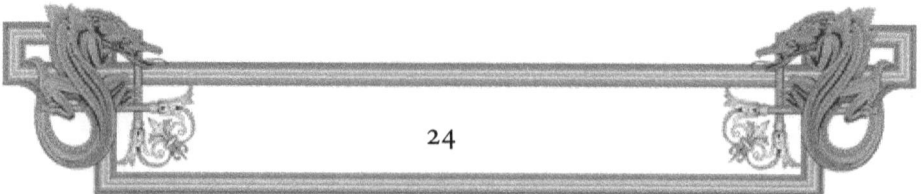

Eternal Recurrence

Everything becomes and recurs eternally – escape is impossible![26]

Metaphysics and religion are becoming less popular in the modern world. Myth, however, still survives, because it entails only a shared past and not a shared religious belief. Myth exists as the ghost or shadow of an expired religion. The use of myth does not, therefore, necessarily entail any connection to a living or contemporaneous religious tradition. Moreover, there is no compulsion or requirement to possess a religious belief in order to accept the cultural significance or validity of a myth. Myth itself is super-historical, and a society which has destroyed its mythology has not only severed itself from its own heritage, but also aborted its present culture. Though Nietzsche is any enemy of religion, he is not immune to the charms of resorting to mythological imagery. As Cristiano Grottanelli states, Nietzsche sought to create a "mythos of the future":

In his reconsideration of Nietzsche's attitude to myth that was published in 1979, Peter Putz (*Der Mythos bei Nietzsche*) stated that the German philosopher stopped discussing myth as such after *Die Ursprung der Tragodie*, only to "fashion a myth (the myth of Life)." More recently still, Alan Megill has stated that Nietzsche created "the mythos of the future," the myth destined to save us from the nihilism that he believes has cast its shadow on Western culture.[27]

---

[26] NIETZSCHE, F., *The Will to Power*, KAUFMANN, W., ed. (New York: Vintage Books, 1968), 545.

[27] GROTTANELLI, C., "Nietzsche and Myth" in *History of Religions*, vol. 36, no.

Therefore, although Nietzsche's ideas departed from those of his predecessors in Germanic Philhellenism, his goal remained the same: cultural reinvigoration. By supplying people with new myths (which maintain links with their ancient predecessors), a culture can be restored, because it unifies individuals under a shared aegis of communal ancestry. Citizens can then develop an identity within the community. To a certain extent, a shared communal experience is necessary for society to function, for a civilization where the citizens are divided is one where loyalties are divided. As Birns reminds us,

> [i]n medieval societies the prevalent virtue is loyalty. Therefore, the question is not "who am I?" but "to whom am I loyal," i.e., "to whom do I pledge allegiance?" Identity is the direct result of that allegiance. Society is then divided into groups, which interlock but at the same time remain separate.[28]

The most apparent reworking of myth in Nietzsche's writing is the manifestation of his prophet Zarathustra, who is no longer an Iranian monotheist but reborn as a prophet and herald, the veritable antithesis of banal monotheism. Beyond good and evil, it is Nietzsche's Zarathustra who acts as the mouthpiece to announce the eventual emergence of Nietzsche's 'Antichrist,' but is not *the* Antichrist himself, who remains Dionysus. It is in *Thus Spoke Zarathustra* that the reader finds mythology used the most, and it is where the fundamental idea of an *eternal recurrence*, delivered in Sphinx-like riddles and parables, is defined. It appears consistently in Nietzsche's other works as well, and if Nietzsche had remained healthy, he would have eventually explained this topic more fully. Unfortunately, this never eventuated, and since Nietzsche himself

---

4, 7-8.

[28] BIRNS, N., "Ressentiment and Counter-Ressentiment: Nietzsche, Scheler, and the Reaction Against Equality," *Nietzsche Circle*, www.nietzschecircle.com/RessentimentMaster.pdf, 15.

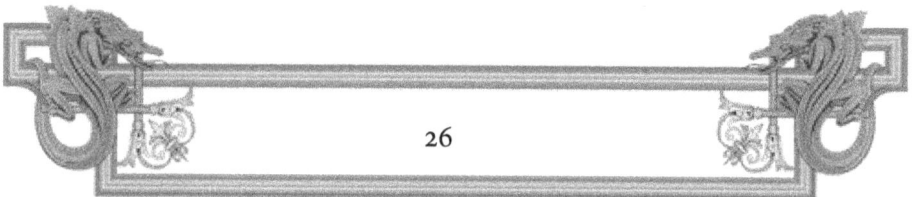

was never able to offer eternal recurrence's exact definition, its meaning remains open to speculation. As such, the only viable means to attempt a description of eternal recurrence is to examine the mythology and philosophy which inspired it. It is obvious from its name that eternal recurrence deals with time, but there is a deeper meaning, shrouded and veiled by centuries of tradition.

Eternal recurrence is connected to the concept of cyclical time, as opposed to the current prevailing notion of linear time, in which the infinite expansion of progress and evolution is postulated. Cyclical time, which is found in both Hinduism and European pre-Christian religions, instead understands time as cyclical and progress as finite, since once a certain point in time is reached, a society regresses into a decayed state, only to one day arise anew.

Eternal recurrence did not develop in a vacuum. It is well-known that Nietzsche, despite his contentions with the predominant religious doctrines of his own era, was very much inspired by Hellenic myths. This period of Hellenic revival was quite popular before Nietzsche composed his main works, and its intellectual prefiguring can be found in the Romantic movement, as well as in other authors such as Creuzer and Bachofen. Creuzer's *Symbolik und Mythologie der alten Völker* includes numerous depictions of nature or time as a cycle, describing Chronos (the ancient Greek personification of time) as "the god who is withdrawn [*zurückgezogen*] into himself," and who was represented by a serpent in the form of a circle. Furthermore, the notion of cyclic time in Creuzer's work also references the Greek idea of *metempsychosis*, which is analogous to reincarnation. Creuzer linked this concept to the god Dionysus as well, since Dionysus – through his death and rebirth – is a symbol of eternal life. This is part of the Eleusinian mysteries, as Nietzsche explains:

The initiates in the Eleusinian mysteries hoped for a rebirth of Dionysus, which we now can understand as the mysterious end

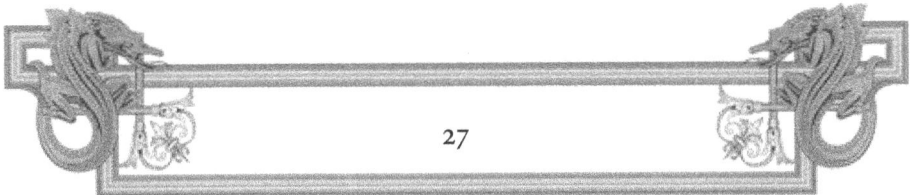

of individuation. The initiate's song of jubilation cried out to this approaching third Dionysus. And only with this hope was there a ray of joy on the face of the fragmented world, torn apart into individuals, just as myth reveals in the picture of the eternal sorrow of sunken Demeter, who rejoices again for the first time when someone says to her that she might be able once again to give birth to Dionysus.[29]

Like time, Dionysus' nature is inherently cyclical, which connects Nietzsche's conception of Dionysus with the notion of eternal recurrence. The idea of an eternal return likewise stems from Bachofen, as it was Bachofen's idea of an eternal return (*ewige Zurückkehr*) to the same point through the cycle of opposites which most closely resembles Nietzsche's concept of eternal recurrence (*ewige Wiederkunft/Wiederkehr*). Bachofen associated his eternal return with several symbols later associated with eternal recurrence, including the caduceus, the phoenix, and the serpent, the latter of which "has a long life, turns back [*zurückkehrt*] from an old one into a youth and gains new and greater powers, until she is resolved [*aufgelöst*] into herself again after the completion of a set span... [S]he is immortal and turns back on herself."[30] Schelling's circle of "eternal recommencing" (*ewiges Wiederbeginnen*) also has a haunting similarity to eternal recurrence (*ewige Wiederkunft/Wiederkehr*), as is seen in the following: "time [...] always devouring itself and always giving birth to itself again [...] continually perishing in its own flames and rejuvenating itself from the ash."[31]

---

[29] NIETZSCHE, F., *The Birth of Tragedy* (Arlington, VA: Richer Resources, 2009).

[30] YELLE, R. A., "The Rebirth of Myth? Nietzsche's Eternal Recurrence and its Romantic Antecedents" in *NUMEN*, vol. 47, 189.

[31] Ibid., 191.

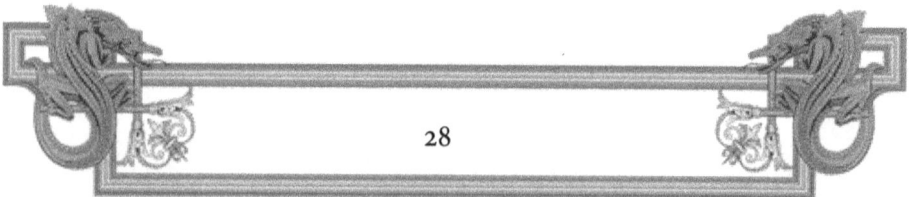

The symbols of the caduceus, phoenix, and serpent are immediately recognizable to anyone familiar with the iconography of myths. The caduceus is the representation of the Hermetic ascent via the solar and lunar powers from the Telluric to the Uranic as the final *hieros gamos* or apotheosis, which signifies mastery of both Heaven and Earth. As such, the phoenix (or eagle, as we see in Nietzsche's work) is the Uranic and the Telluric is the serpent power. For both Creuzer and Bachofen, the events of cosmic time shifted and revolved around the twin polarities of Heaven and Earth, shaping the course of both history and civilization. As such, it is no coincidence that they are the animal companions of Nietzsche's prophet, Zarathustra.[32] Zarathustra mentions his animal totems as being an eagle and a serpent: "An eagle soared through the sky in wide circles, and on him there hung a serpent, not like prey but like a friend: for she kept herself wound around his neck." The snake and the eagle are thus conjoined, not in opposition.[33] In addition to being esoteric symbols and poetic metaphors, the eagle and the serpent have yet another purpose for Nietzsche: they represent cultural forces that he refers to as super-historical, and thus serve to connect Zarathustra's actions with Nietzsche's early work, *On the Use and Abuse of History for Life*.

Even at this stage of his literary career, many of Nietzsche's ideas can already be found here in a rudimentary form. The unhistorical is the average man. Although he is referred to here as a 'beast,' it is easy to see this beast evolving to become the 'Herd' in Nietzsche's later writings: "Thus the beast lives *unhistorically*, for it gets up in the

---

[32] Not to be confused with the Iranian Zarathustra, who reduced 'Heaven' and 'Earth' to the battle of 'good' vs. 'evil,' ultimately leading to Christian monotheism – both of which Nietzsche was opposed to.

[33] Another author – also inspired by Bachofen – is Julius Evola, who promoted purely the Uranic pole, to his own detriment. Life cannot exist without Earth, and Evola's misunderstanding of the Chthonic or Telluric aspect in esotericism is one of his greatest flaws.

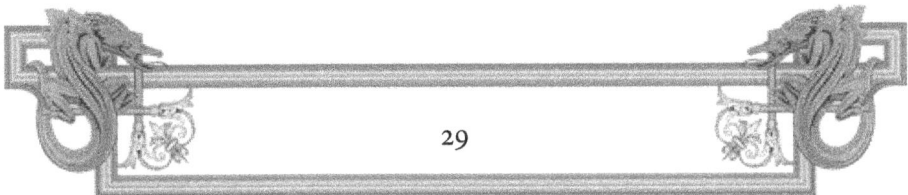

present like a number without any odd fraction left over; it does not know how to play a part, hides nothing, and appears in each moment exactly and entirely what it is."[34] The unhistorical is then contrasted with the super-historical:

> With the phrase "the unhistorical" I designate the art and the power of being able to forget and to enclose oneself in a horizon with borders; "super-historical" I call the powers which divert the gaze from what is developing back to what gives existence an eternal and unchanging character, to art and religion.[35]

The super-historical therefore exists in a manner similar to Jung's concept of psychoids: they exist outside of the human lifespan and act on the subconscious nature of humanity, but have an independent existence exterior to it. The super-historical thus denotes forces beyond the sphere of human control, save when in the hands of fictional prophets such as Zarathustra. It is via recourse to the super-historical that one can influence or remain unaffected by the effects of time and history. The super-historical provides a reference to an eternal mode of art and religion (the Primordial Tradition). This paradigm harkens back to older surviving elements of culture such as myth, which serve to provide anchors in Nietzsche's 'mind-war' against the 'cultural philistines.'[36] Because forces such as myth, art, and religion are super-historical, their recurrence is certain, and they have the power to shape the present in their pure, eternal, and unconditional state, which lies rooted in the primordial past. Eternal recurrence is not just a methodical use of Dionysus and the Ouroboros; it is also tied to Nietzsche's perception of history. It

---

[34] NIETZSCHE, F., *On the Use and Abuse of History for Life* (1874), trans. JOHNSTON, I. C., *http://individual.utoronto.ca/bmclean/hermeneutics/nietzsche_suppl/N_use_abuse_01.htm*

[35] Ibid.

[36] Nietzsche's 'mind war' will be explained in a later chapter.

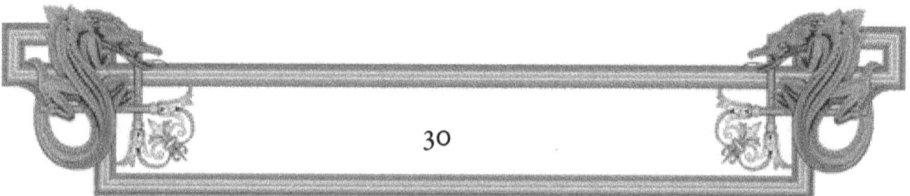

implies that super-historical temporal forces are cyclic, although – as per Heraclitus – one does not step into the same stream twice. The stream may change its essence, but this does not negate the course of its flow. Thus time, to Nietzsche, is not strictly cyclic, but more akin to a spiral. The pattern repeats, but there are deviations; one can step into it, but each occurrence will never be an exact repetition. Nietzsche states this directly by comparing the linear notion of time to that of cyclic time in *Zarathustra* when he confronts the dwarf who represents the Spirit of Gravity:

> "Behold this gateway, dwarf!" I continued. "It has two faces. Two paths meet here; no one has yet followed either to its end. This long lane stretches back for an eternity. And the long lane out there, that is another eternity. They contradict each other, these paths; they offend each other face to face, and it is here at this gateway that they come together. The name of the gateway is inscribed above: 'Moment.' But whoever would follow one of them, on and on, farther and farther — do you believe, dwarf, that these paths contradict each other eternally?" "All that is straight lies," the dwarf murmured contemptuously. "All truth is crooked; time itself is a circle."[37]

The dwarf presents Zarathustra with the fact that the two paths are one, and the illusion that there are two paths is a lie. The dwarf's statement reveals the nature of the cyclical to Zarathustra. This is not exactly a joyous revelation, however, hence why the dwarf/Spirit of Gravity is chosen to unveil the nature of time in the narrative. One of Nietzsche's most profound statements on time also deals with eternal recurrence and the horror of an endlessly repeated act or moment:

---

[37] YELLE, "The Rebirth of Myth?," 180.

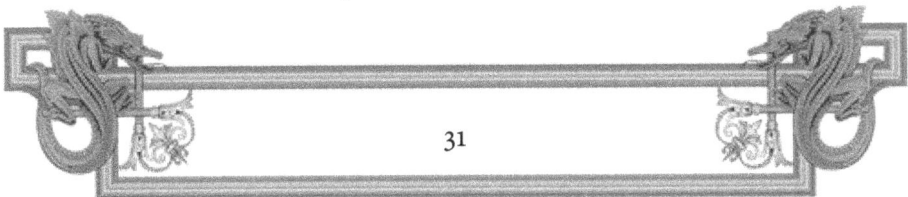

What, if some day or night a demon were to steal after you into your loneliest loneliness and say to you: "This life as you now live it and have lived it, you will have to live once more and innumerable times more; and there will be nothing new in it, but every pain and every joy and every thought and sigh and everything unutterably small or great in your life will have to return to you, all in the same succession and sequence"... Would you not throw yourself down and gnash your teeth and curse the demon who spoke thus? Or have you once experienced a tremendous moment when you would have answered him: 'You are a god and never have I heard anything more divine.'[38]

This repetition of an endless moment follows closely from the previously mentioned metempsychosis of the Greeks, and is probably better explained to a modern Western audience as reincarnation. We also find traditional references to it in the teachings of Hinduism and the notion of *samsara*. In terms of Nietzsche's own work, it is linked to pre-determinism of his simple but effective *amor fati* formula for happiness. Here, however, in the purely logical realm, the endless repetition of a decisive moment which eternally recurs offers us another rule: that every action has a consequence. Until the faulty decision is undone, one is doomed to make the same mistake – not only in this lifetime, but also in any future ones. There is no action without an equal reaction; no energy once dispersed dissipates into entropy devoid of motion. So say the laws of physics, just like the laws of logic, for both are at their core just higher mathematics. As William Blake would say, "the fool who persists in his folly will become wise" – but, according to Nietzsche, this is not so. A fool will persist in his folly until the *unique moment* from which the pattern of his folly stems is broken. *Amor fati*, blessed in the hands of the wise, is devastating for a fool.

---

[38] NIETZSCHE, F., *The Gay Science*, ed. KAUFMANN, W. (New York: Vintage Books, 1974), pp. 273-274.

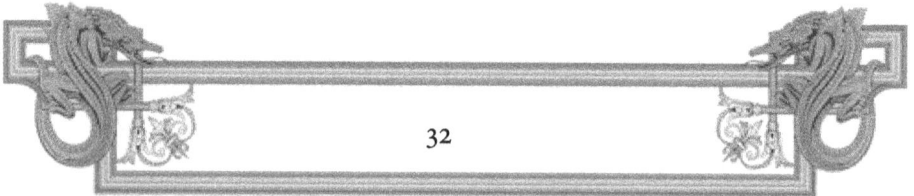

Accordingly, it is not Zarathustra who reveals the secret of eternal recurrence, but his adversary/lower self, the Spirit of Gravity, who tells Zarathustra that "time is a circle." It is not linear but destined to repeat, with time/history always following the same course, in a spiral rotation, with each slight deviation being enough to create an illusion that it is linear. Bruce Detwiler traces Nietzsche's use of recurrence back to Heraclitus, stating that "[t]he doctrine of the 'eternal recurrence,' that is, of the unconditional and infinitely repeated circular course of things – this doctrine of Zarathustra might, in the end, have been taught already by Heraclitus."[39] In a direct paraphrasing of Heraclitus, Nietzsche states that Heraclitus' stream is indeed circular. In the guise of an Ouroboros, the serpent bites its own tail, meaning that it is in a spiral rotation, thus becoming an infinite creature with no beginning or end that ultimately devours itself, ceaselessly:

Do not be afraid of the stream of things: this stream turns back on itself: it runs away from itself, not only twice. Every "it was" becomes again an "it is." The past bites everything future in the tail.[40]

Other references to the Ouroboros are less explicit, such as Zarathustra's caduceus, "a staff with a golden handle on which a serpent is coiled around the sun."[41] The Ouroboros, despite the serpent being a symbol of the Telluric powers, is a symbol of spiritual ascension and mastery. When coiled, the Ouroboros serpent is a spiral, which represents the passage of time, or more specifically the measurement of time created by the circular orbit of the Earth around the Sun. The Ouroboros symbolizes 'time' because

---

39   YELLE, "The Rebirth of Myth?," 178.

40   Ibid., 180.

41   Ibid., 182.

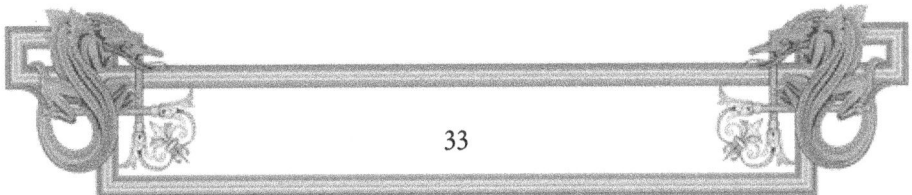

it represents the rotation of the Earth around the Sun – and thanks to the discoveries of science, it proves that time, as least as humanity measures it, is indeed circular.

Eternal recurrence is not merely a man-made supposition grafted atop a cosmological event, however. It is something more than that. Nor does it directly pertain to the Spirit of Gravity, which prevents the human ascent to a higher type. It is the super-historical reborn, the revolution of time and eternity, which repeats endlessly in every single moment. Time becomes an inevitable and eternal construct that pervades every aspect of consciousness until the mind is liberated and 'freed' from the repetition of the cycle.

This rebirth or recurrence of myth provides the impetus which enables culture to flourish, as sculpted by the Dionysian artist/ philosopher who functions as a 'physician of culture.' Dionysus, in particular, is a symbol of cultural transition for Nietzsche. Tracy B. Strong iterates this sentiment when he states that "Nietzsche's appeal to the Dionysian does not refer to an attempt to go back to something that lies under Greek life or the origins of that which is Greek but, rather, to more new developments that might serve in the transformation of the older Apollonian world."[42] Dionysus, therefore, acts as a super-historical symbol which links the past to the future. Accordingly, myth then becomes a powerful weapon for the preservation of culture, because unlike religion, belief in the literal truth of a myth is not required; it is merely a concession that it is part of shared experiences and a testament to the enduring value of history, which serves to convey cultural expressions from antiquity into modern times.

------

[42] STRONG, T. B., "Nietzsche and the Political: Tyranny, Tragedy, Cultural Revolution, and Democracy" in *The Journal of Nietzsche Studies*, no. 35/36 (Spring/ Autumn 2008), 57.

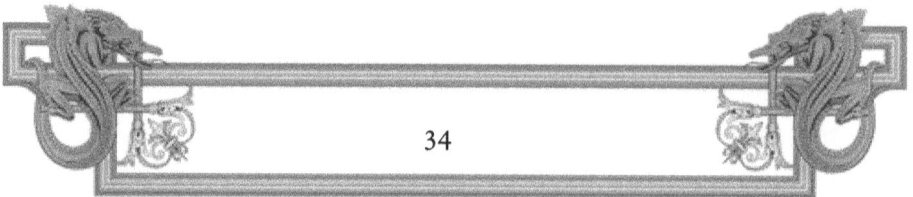

RESSENTIMENT & CHRISTIANITY

Given Nietzsche's fondness for Hellenic mythology, it should come as no surprise that he had little interest in Christianity. Though initially merely critical of the religion, his vehemence towards it intensified as a result of his ill-fated friendship with the composer Richard Wagner, which turned infamously sour. In the beginning, the two amicably discussed music and mythology. However, Wagner revealed a preference for two things which Nietzsche found extremely unpalatable: Christianity and antisemitism. This was further exacerbated by elements in Wagner's music-drama *Parsifal*, which ultimately led Nietzsche to write *Nietzsche contra Wagner*, as well as Nietzsche's ultimate attack on Christianity, *The Antichrist*.

To understand Nietzsche's animosity towards Christianity, it entails not only examining the issues surrounding his friendship with Wagner, but also the intimate relation between the super-historical nature of myth and human culture. This linking of the destruction of myth with the collapse of civilization can be found in Nietzsche as far back as *The Birth of Tragedy*, where he writes that

> [t]hese same symptoms lead us to suspect the same lack at the heart of this culture – the destruction of myth. It seems hardly

possible that transplanting a foreign myth would enjoy any lasting success, without irreparably damaging the tree in the transplant.[1]

If myth, then, is the heart of culture, which can be eroded by foreign influences that are not even beneficial to the myth being propagated, what is Nietzsche suggesting as the cause of Europe's cultural destruction? His answer is not subtle, and is strongly implied by *The Antichrist*'s title. For Nietzsche, Christianity was the principal cause of the Roman civilization's decline.

Moreover, Nietzsche's unfavorable views regarding Christianity were exacerbated by his contact with Richard Wagner. Wagner's influence over German culture through music was immense, and Nietzsche most certainly disagreed with many of his ideas. The first point of disagreement between them concerned Wagner's antisemitism[2] and the second was Christianity. Nietzsche's inevitable bitter dispute with Wagner was due to the latter's increasing incorporation of Christianity into his late work – a belief system which Nietzsche considered absurd. Nietzsche also considered it as contradictory, since Wagner was also antisemitic. Therefore, any analysis of Nietzsche's transition from the study of myth to increasingly vehement attacks on Christianity has to commence by providing the background of Nietzsche's interactions with Wagner.

During their friendship, they corresponded heavily regarding the creation of new mythologies, reworking Hellenic and Nordic myths to promote their own respective ideas. Wagner drew heavily on Nordic mythology in his music-dramas, and had grandiose aims

---

[1] NIETZSCHE, F., *The Birth of Tragedy* (Arlington, VA: Richer Resources, 2009).

[2] This was quite mainstream in Nietzsche's time. Wagner was just one of many with such a prejudice in Germany, but he had greater influence than most due to his fame.

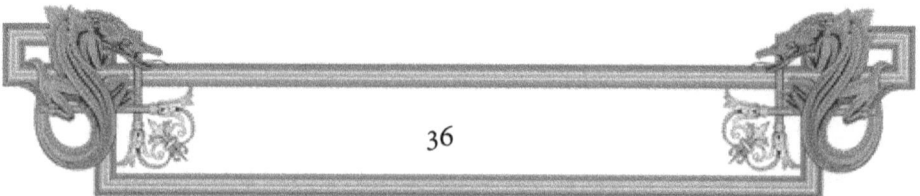

for his work beyond mere artistic endeavor. In *Deutsche Kunst und Deutsche Politik* (*German Art and German Politics*), he wrote about the social and political meaning of the aesthetic theories he was developing: "Modern life [...shall be] reorganized by the rebirth of art, and especially by a new theater whose life-giving function shall be equal to that of ancient Greek drama."[3] Although Nietzsche's friendship with Wagner eventually ended as a result of the musician's religious views, initially he also explored the uses of myth during the period of their acquaintance, and they found commonality between their ideas.

Wagner's manipulation of myth through music and drama had a profound impact upon Germany, and the influence he exerted over the country as a result of his fame was likewise significant. Although Nietzsche passionately disagreed with Wagner's antisemitism, he nevertheless agreed that culture should be the driving impetus behind the political change. Yet, in the end, he could not accept the sort of culture that Wagner desired and opted to create his own instead, which eventually led to the publication of *Nietzsche contra Wagner*. Nietzsche also briefly revisited the problem of Wagner's antisemitism in *The Antichrist*, where he writes that "Jews have so utterly misled humanity that today still Christians may have anti-Semitic feelings, without understanding themselves as the ultimate consequence of Judaism."[4] This is a not so subtle jibe at Wagner and other Christians who were advocating antisemitism in Germany at the time.

Although Nietzsche was not antisemitic, he was anti-Christian. Moreover, his views on Christianity cannot be examined in isolation from Judaism, as the Old Testament is indisputably a Christian

---

[3]   GROTTANELLI, C., "Nietzsche and Myth" in *History of Religions* (August 1997), 3.

[4]   Ibid., 7.

text derived from the older tradition. As a consequence, there is considerable overlap between Christianity and Judaism, especially when one considers that Yahweh is the supreme deity of both traditions. It is precisely here, at the periphery betwixt Judaism and Christianity, that Nietzsche brings his concept of the 'slave revolt' into play. The Jews and Romans represent the master morality, and the Christians, as the lower caste in both Rome and Judea, embody the 'slave morality'. The 'slave revolt' enacted by the first Christians laid the foundation for the fall of Rome and all the historical consequences that followed from it. Thus, for Nietzsche, it is not the Jews but the Christians who are at the root of the modern world's problem. Nevertheless, in his philosophy it is impossible to divorce Christianity from its older parent religion. This is, in fact, where Nietzsche's 'slave revolt' hypothesis begins.

In Nietzsche's rendition of history, Christians are portrayed as the low-caste branch of Judaism, and the Jews instigate the overthrow of the Roman Empire by sowing political *ressentiment* among the lower classes of society – the Christians. In *On the Genealogy of Morality*, for example, Nietzsche describes the slave revolt in morality as the struggle of "'Rome against Judea, Judea against Rome':—there has hitherto been no greater event than this struggle, this question, this deadly contradiction."[5] This single incident, by Nietzsche's reckoning, had a devastating impact on European history.

This is also why Nietzsche spoke more favorably of Judaism than Christianity: for Nietzsche, the early Christians were the low-caste people of Judea, meaning that Jews possessed a 'master morality', as did the Romans. According to Nietzsche, because they had this master morality, the Jews were able to manipulate early Christianity and use it as a political tool. For Nietzsche, then, the Jews had

[5] SCHOTTEN, C. H., *Nietzsche's Revolution: Décadence, Politics, and Sexuality* (New York: Palgrave Macmillan, 2009), 99.

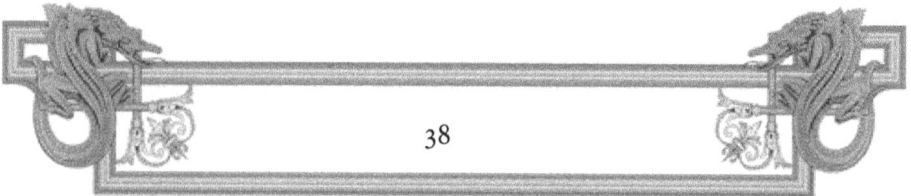

a stronger Will to Power than the Christians. As such, he views Christianity's creation as a 'Holy Lie' deployed as an act of political sabotage to weaken the Roman Empire and its cultural values from within. The paradox is that although Nietzsche admired the Jews, he did so because they enacted a "secret black art of truly grand politics of revenge, of a farseeing, subterranean, slowly advancing, and premeditated revenge."[6] Thus, although Nietzsche respected the Jews, the source of his respect is due to the strength of their Will to Power, mendacious tenacity, and Machiavellian prowess – and because they did not share the characteristics of meekness and forgiveness which are predominant in Christianity. Detwiler states that this occurs because "the noble type is powerful, the slave – and all those who are downtrodden and full of resentment – proclaims the blessedness of the meek."[7] Moreover, according to Nietzsche, slave morality arose from an inversion of aristocratic values:

[…] saying the wretched alone are the good; the poor, impotent, lowly alone are the good; the suffering, deprived, sick, ugly alone are pious, alone are blessed by God […] and you the powerful and noble, are on the contrary the evil, the cruel […] the godless to all eternity; and you shall be in all eternity the unblessed, accursed, and damned. (GM I7)[8]

However, despite Nietzsche's admiration for the Jews, he also criticized them for creating Christianity. This becomes more apparent when Nietzsche cites differences between the Semitic and

---

[6] WALLACE, R. J., "Ressentiment, Value, and Self-Vindication: Making Sense of Nietzsche's Slave Revolt" *Nietzsche and Morality*, ed. LEITER, B. & SINHABABU, N., (Oxford: Oxford University Press, 2009), 19.

[7] DETWILER, B., *Nietzsche and the Politics of Aristocratic Radicalism* (Chicago: University of Chicago Press, 1990), 121.

[8] DOMBOWSKY, D., *Nietzsche's Machiavellian Politics* (New York: Palgrave Macmillan, 2004), 48.

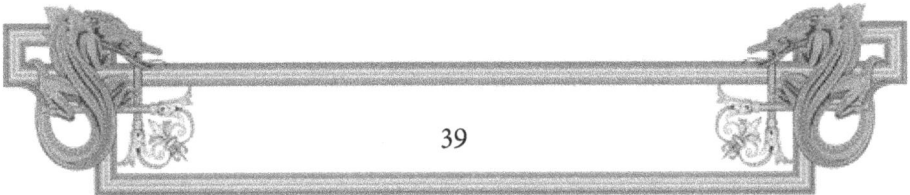

'Aryan'[9] mythos; in particular, the story of the Fall of Man. Citing different descriptions of the Fall, Nietzsche writes that the

> [...] legend of Prometheus[10] is indigenous to the entire community of Aryan races and attests to their prevailing talent for profound and tragic vision. It is not improbable that this myth has the same characteristic importance for the Aryan mind as the myth of the Fall has for the Semitic, and that the two myths are related as brother and sister.[11]

While they appear to be in opposition, the use of 'Aryan' here is flawed, and there is no opposition between the 'Aryan' and 'Semitic' races as such a racial distinction never existed in the ancient world. Nevertheless, there is a religious distinction to be made, as Nietzsche believed that "the Semites attribute sin to the female gender, and it is quite consistent with these notions that the original act of *hubris* should be attributed to man, original sin to a woman."[12] The Biblical 'original sin' is, therefore, different from Hellenic 'original

---

[9] The word 'Aryan' was used here in the context of Nietzsche's era, which has long since been discredited. The quotation marks are used to denote that in this period of history, views concerning who and what was 'Aryan' were largely incorrect. There was never any Aryan invasion of India, and they were not of a 'pale skinned, blue-eyed, and blond' ethnic phenotype. The name *Āryan* comes from the word *ārya* (noble) and is a caste/class term, not a racial one. It originates from India.

[10] The Greek Titan Prometheus represents the ancient Greek sin of *hybris* (hubris, pride). For this sin, and his defiance of Zeus, Prometheus is chained to a rock and his liver is eaten repeatedly for all eternity by an eagle, after which it always grows back (the Greeks believed that the liver was the center of the soul, hence its use in hepatomancy, a barbaric form of fortune telling involving animal sacrifice that was imported to Greece and Rome from the Middle East as a result of the influences of the 'Persian Magi' and an erroneous belief in their spiritual prowess). The eagle is the symbol of Zeus' Uranic power over the inferior Titans.

[11] GROTTANELLI, "Nietzsche and Myth," 1.

[12] Ibid., 2.

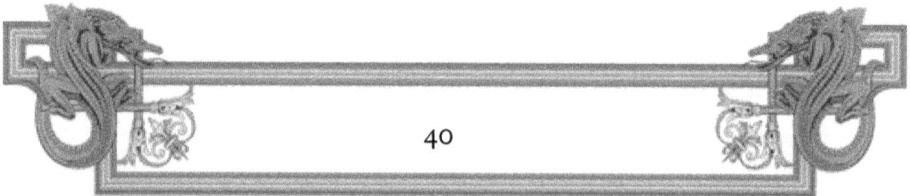

sin.' Nietzsche's description of the opposition between the two is nonetheless an intriguing illustration of the religious differences between the Jews and the Greeks in antiquity. The origin of sin for the Greeks is Promethean hubris (*hybris*) or narcissism, whereas for the Jewish faith, it is obtaining the knowledge that belongs exclusively to Yahweh by eating the forbidden fruit. According to Nietzsche, Christianity and all its political heirs stand as an inversion of these values, for Christianity constitutes a reaction against the morality of privilege, and "the victory of Chandala values, the evangel preached to the poor and lowly, the collective rebellion of everything downtrodden."[13]

Furthermore, Nietzsche believes that Christianity's cultural implications still linger on in contemporary politics. For Nietzsche, the "[s]ecular imperatives derived from Christian morality, filled the void left by the impending collapse of Christianity"[14] by shifting from the religious directive to a more political one. In *Beyond Good and Evil*, Nietzsche accuses Christianity of being the progenitor of almost every wrong idea in Western politics, declaring that "[t]he democratic movement is the heir of the Christian movement."[15] One has to remember that democracy and its inherent Left/Right partisan split was a recent innovation in Nietzsche's time, and not the commonplace dichotomy it has become today, where no one is capable of imaging a life without democracy. Nietzsche's generation had been raised in a society based on aristocracy and hierarchy. As such, when he speaks ill of democracy, this was not revolutionary for his era; it was the norm, and many people were skeptical of this radical new political innovation.

---

[13] DOMBOWSKY, *Nietzsche's Machiavellian Politics*, 62.

[14] DETWILER, *Nietzsche and the Politics of Aristocratic Radicalism*, 131.

[15] Ibid., 129.

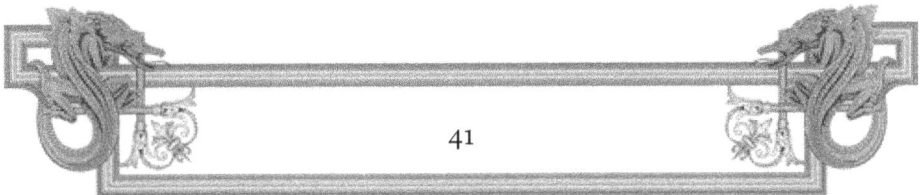

Moreover, Nietzsche's hostility to democracy does not arise from a fondness for what would eventually become German fascism,[16] but because he believes democracy erodes all notions of hierarchy, and, consequently also weakens his theory of the Will to Power. Socialism, in particular, is seen by Nietzsche as the closest to Christian sentiment. Thus socialism is treated with the same disdain that Nietzsche held for antisemitism, demonstrating that he was not ideologically comfortable with either the Right or the Left. Nietzsche states that "residues of Christian value judgments are found everywhere in socialistic and positivistic systems" and that "the entire socialist ideal" is "nothing but a clumsy misunderstanding of that Christian ideal." Nietzsche also believes that "the democratic movement is the heir of the Christian movement,"[17] which leaves no margin for error in misinterpreting his political views. Nietzsche's opinions on politics, however, reach even beyond this, for he "views the anarchist, democratic, and socialist movements as the successors of the Christian movement, as neo-Christian and, accordingly, the militant European worker or proletariat, as an avatar of Christian 'anarchist agitation in the Empire' (A 58)."[18] Thus, Nietzsche believed that Christianity had

> forged out of the *ressentiment* of the masses its chief weapon against us, against everything noble [...] The aristocratic outlook has been undermined most deeply by the lie of equality of souls [...] the belief in the 'prerogative of the majority.'[19]

---

[16] Fascism began as a democratic movement, since its leaders such as Hitler and Mussolini were democratically elected.

[17] SCHOTTEN, *Nietzsche's Revolution*, 101.

[18] DOMBOWSKY, *Nietzsche's Machiavellian Politics*, 12.

[19] Ibid., 20.

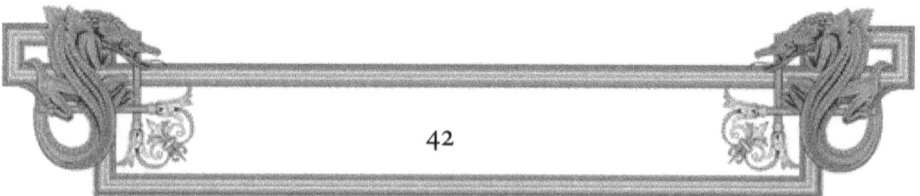

According to Nietzsche, the problem does not purely lie with the Christians. Rather, the *décadence* is inherent in the entire priest caste, and results from the dispersion of *ressentiment* that in turn allows them to rule. Nietzsche is not coy about his preference for the warrior caste, whom he views as more honest and noble. In *Genealogy*, Nietzsche makes it clear that these two factions of the nobility – the warriors and priests – compete for political power.[20] However, even though the warrior caste has greater physical strength, the priest caste still attains power, and it is via the acquiescence of the stronger that they are enabled to do so. In response, Nietzsche asks, "What gives authority when one does not have physical power in one's hands?"[21] It is the concept of the Holy Lie that enables one to do rule vicariously over the other castes, and this is why Nietzsche classifies them as decadent. The Holy Lie is a process of deception that makes promises eternally but never fulfills them, beguiling the common people with notions such as the afterlife and salvation, whilst at the same frightening them into submission with the non-existent punishments of Hell for sins against the hierarchical order. The priest can only rule because others believe in the supernatural; the warrior – who is more honest – rules through more easily palpable means. But there is a problem with this conclusion: Nietzsche himself does not always appear to be an atheist. He utilizes themes drawn from Hellenic mythology, endorses the Hindu *Laws of Manu*, and even refers to himself (albeit through a multitude of riddles) as the Antichrist.[22] Thus, his postulates can be challenged by two factors.

Firstly, even though Nietzsche himself does not support supernatural concepts, they enter into his work through mythological themes.

---

[20] REGINSTER, "Nietzsche on Ressentiment and Valuation" in *Philosophy and Phenomenological Research*, Vol. 57, No. 2 (June 1997), 285.

[21] DOMBOWSKY, *Nietzsche's Machiavellian Politics*, 155.

[22] This will be explained in the next chapter.

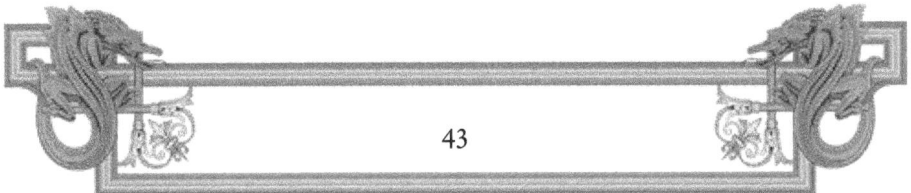

Many of Nietzsche's ideas are pronounced by his fictional priest-prophet, Zarathustra. Secondly, philosophers themselves rule ideologically in a fashion similar to that of priests – and what is a philosophy save a religion devoid of its spiritual elements? The two approaches are nearly identical. Thus, the priest and the philosopher are both decadent, according to Nietzsche's own standard, which is a self-made trap that Nietzsche, regrettably, stumbles directly into. But then even this could be deliberate: for the priest caste, would it not be best to pronounce that the warriors are superior so that they fight and die to protect their intellectual leaders? This would also count as a Holy Lie, and is just one example of the way in which the priest can rule over the warrior: *by having the genius to adopt the secondary role.* Unfortunately, the same adage could well hold true for the entire philosophical profession.

Returning to the implications of Christianity as a deliberately orchestrated rebellion against Roman authority, it is the priest caste which initiates the slave revolt, for, as Nietzsche insists,

> the slave does not create values, a privilege which belongs exclusively to the masters (cf. BGE, 261). The slave, Nietzsche suggests, blindly accepts his master's values – and this is, arguably, what makes him a 'slave' (in the psychological sense) in the first place.[23]

This state of psychological slavery arises from *ressentiment.* *Ressentiment* is another crucial concept in Nietzsche's philosophy. *Ressentiment* is a form of resentment arising from envy, where a mass of those who believe themselves to be oppressed attempt to reform the social structure in accordance with their interests, overthrowing those who are identified as the governing elite. As R. Jay Wallace explains, "*Ressentiment* becomes creative and gives birth

---

[23] REGINSTER, "Nietzsche on Ressentiment," 289.

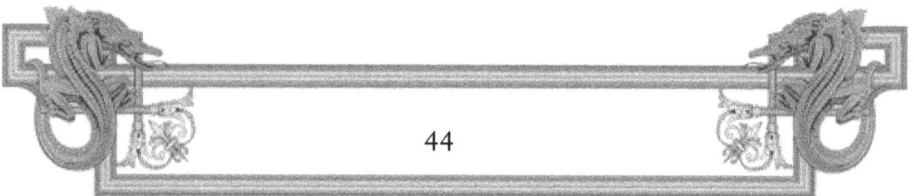

to values when the tensions that attend it lead the powerless to adopt and internalize a wholly new evaluative framework."[24] Slave morality not only creates *ressentiment*, but it also creates a state of despair. *Ressentiment* represents "the repression of 'all that represents the ascending movement of life, well constitutedness, power, beauty, self-affirmation on earth.'"[25] Rather than raising oneself to a higher level in order to replace the ruling powers, those possessed by *ressentiment* instead opt to bring the superior individuals down. It thus represents a destructive negative impulse, as opposed to a genuine positive emanation of the Will to Power. Bernard Reginster believes that in Nietzsche's view,

> the 'man of *ressentiment*' is weak, but not weakwilled. He is weak because he does not have what it takes to realize his values, not because he lacks the will to pursue them. His will is, on the contrary, prodigiously strong, so strong indeed that it is not even altered by his conviction that he is too weak to fulfill its demands. But unlike the weakwilled individual, he becomes fundamentally confused about his values. His professed values are merely apparent and adopted as covert means to realize his repressed (real) desires.[26]

Furthermore, according to Reginster, the political form of *ressentiment* arises from "'the man of *ressentiment*' who is 'corrupted' because he lacks the integrity of self, a trait Nietzsche regards as essential to 'nobility' of character."[27] The man of *ressentiment*, unable to procure a means of obtaining power based on merit, succumbs to *décadence*. He becomes weak, insipid, and envious of all who do

---

[24] WALLACE, "Ressentiment, Value, and Self-Vindication," 13.

[25] DOMBOWSKY, *Nietzsche's Machiavellian Politics*, 16.

[26] REGINSTER, "Nietzsche on Ressentiment and Valuation," 294.

[27] Ibid., 283.

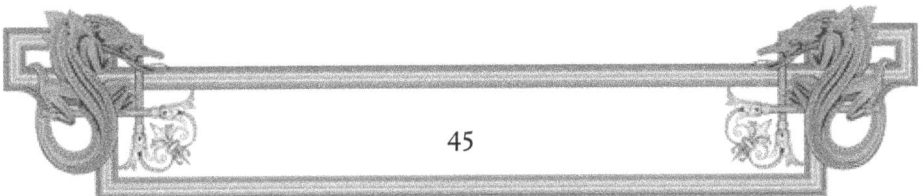

better than him. Instead of raising himself to a level where he can compete as an equal, the man of *ressentiment* attacks all who are doing better than himself. Out of spite, he demands a great 'leveling' and seeks to bring all his competitors down to his own level.

Political *ressentiment* occurs where this is taken beyond relations between individuals and is directed at entire demographic groups. Under such psychologically adverse conditions, for the man of *ressentiment*, who is in the grip of slave morality, there are only two logical outcomes: apathy or revolt. However, the slave who does not revolt and succumbs to indifference truly becomes a slave, for he or she accepts the abysmal status prescribed by the masters. As such, the state of slavery is dependent upon a subconscious choice of obeisance, and a slave who openly revolts is healthier than one who submissively accepts his or her role. In this specific case of the Romans, however, it is the Jewish priest caste who initiated the revolt by sowing *ressentiment* amongst the Christians. It is they who invert the value tables to destroy the Roman Empire. As to why this slave revolt remains imperceptible to many when we read today's history books, it is difficult to discern "precisely because it has been victorious."[28]

---

[28] WALLACE, "Ressentiment, Value, and Self-Vindication," 6.

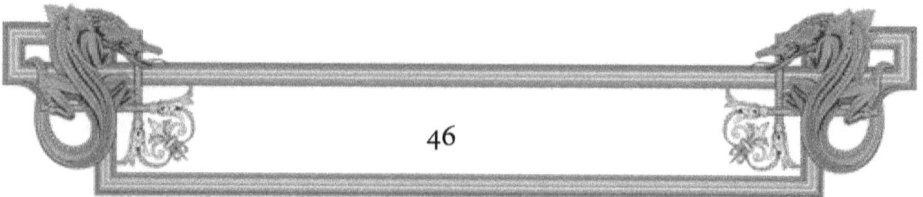

The Death of God

The concept of the slave revolt which, according to Nietzsche, has poisoned the Western world for two thousand years, is not his only divergence into religious philosophy. The idea for which he is most renowned is his grand proclamation that "God is dead." On the surface, this sounds simple enough; however, in a Lovecraftian twist, this is much more complex than it appears to be, and apparently, "That is not dead which can eternal lie." Nietzsche's statement that "God is dead," is, of course, well-known; what is lesser-known is the complex chain of references that connect this statement to other critical points within his philosophy. One of these is found in the poem "Ariadne's Lament," in which another concept of Nietzsche's, known as 'the ladder of religious cruelty,'[29] is hinted at. The three rungs of this ladder represent three stages in the development of the sacrifice: in archaic religions, people sacrificed humans to their gods; in times of moral certainty, people sacrificed their strongest drives and instincts to their gods; in a time yet to come, people will sacrifice god himself (which is representative of any belief in consolation and salvation) as a final act of cruelty against themselves.[30] Even Nietzsche did not fully believe that society was ready to embrace the death of God, and this is described in one of his most famous pieces of writing, 'The Parable of the Madman':

> How shall we comfort ourselves, the murderers of all murderers? *What was holiest and mightiest of all that the world has yet owned has bled to death under our knives: who will wipe this blood off*

---

[29] THEISEN, B., "Rhythms of Oblivion" in *Nietzsche and the Feminine*, ed. BURGARD, P. J. (Charlottesville, VA: University Press of Virginia, 1994), 92.

[30] Ibid., 92.

us? What water is there for us to clean ourselves? What festivals of atonement, what sacred games shall we have to invent? Is not the greatness of this deed too great for us? Must we ourselves not become gods simply to appear worthy of it? There has never been a greater deed; and whoever is born after us – for the sake of this deed he will belong to a higher history than all history hitherto.

Here the madman fell silent and looked again at his listeners; and they, too, were silent and stared at him in astonishment. At last he threw his lantern on the ground, and it broke into pieces and went out. "I have come too early," he said then; "my time is not yet. This tremendous event is still on its way, still wandering; it has not yet reached the ears of men. Lightning and thunder require time; the light of the stars requires time; deeds, though done, still require time to be seen and heard. This deed is still more distant from them than most distant stars – *and yet they have done it themselves.*[31]

Here, the death of God is not portrayed as the glorious victory it should have been. On the contrary, it is anticlimax. The deed has been done, God is dead, but what follows? A fleeting and hollow victory? Humanity is not described here as Nietzsche's higher type who were destined to become god-like, but instead as murderers whose hands are stained with the blood of Nietzsche's own literary crime. God is dead, but the people are not mentally or spiritually strong enough to be capable of living without the *idea* of god. With God 'dead,' humanity is lost; the premature death of God becomes a murder, transformed into a criminal act against humanity rather than its salvation. The death of God thus deviates from Nietzsche's original premise of creating the *Übermensch* and becomes an act of cruelty – not towards God, but towards humanity itself. This ties the murder

---

[31] NIETZSCHE, F., *The Gay Science*, ed. KAUFMANN, W., (New York: Vintage, 1974), 181-82.

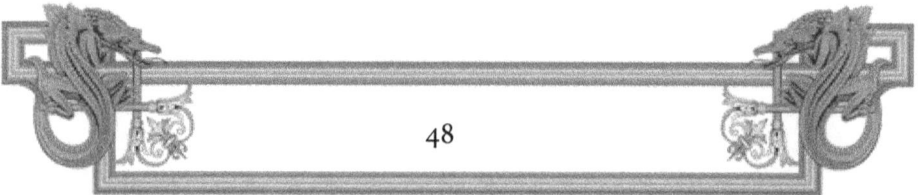

of God to 'the ladder of cruelty': it is an act of cruelty performed by humanity, against humanity. In line with this perspective, Gary Shapiro draws attention to a statement by Nietzsche that connects this act to his political beliefs:

> As Nietzsche had his madman ask why we don't yet smell the odors of God's decomposition, so his analysis of the slow but inevitable decay of the national state points to a parallel decentering in the political sphere. To sum this up: "The belief in a divine order in the realm of politics, in a sacred mystery in the existence of the state, is of religious origin: if religion disappears the state will unavoidably lose its ancient Isis veil and cease to excite reverence."[32]

If Shapiro's statement is correct, then the death of God could lead to nothing more than substituting a political constitution for the Bible, which is most assuredly *not* the outcome Nietzsche desires. Rather than instigating a new incarnation of the Holy Lie, Nietzsche wishes to fill the void left by the death of God with a world presided over by his *Übermensch*. However, it is obvious from the 'Parable of the Madman' that even Nietzsche is pessimistic about this actually occurring. As such, Nietzsche's real intention is not to remove religion entirely. Instead, he attempts to replace it: substituting the Holy Lie of Christianity with one founded on another myth and a new set of values. It is for this reason that he places his words in the mouth of the prophet Zarathustra, praises Dionysus, and draws upon Eastern sources such as the Hindu *Laws of Manu (Manusmṛti)*.

In the *Laws of Manu*, Nietzsche finds an approximation of his ideal political organization: namely, an aristocratic social structure or political regime based on a hierarchical order of rank, or order of

---

[32] SHAPIRO, G., *Nietzsche's Earth: Great Events, Great Politics* (Chicago: The University of Chicago Press, 2016), 70.

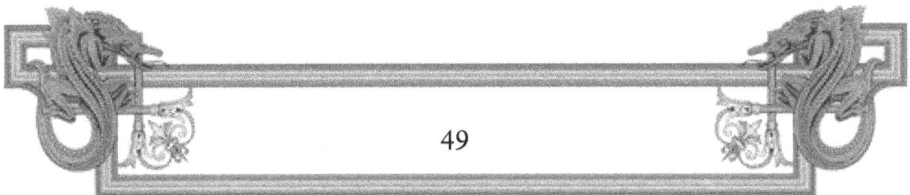

castes, where rights and duties are not shared and is ruled by a noble class. It is the closest instance of a template for the aristocratic society he desires. The *Laws of Manu* presents itself as a discourse given by the sage Manu providing the "guidelines for all the social classes." Nietzsche's interest in this text is also in its religious use. Firstly, he notes the value of Hinduism as being equal in power to the Judeo-Christian Tradition and looks to the Vedic past to create a counter-tradition. In *The Laws of Manu,* he finds a legislative book similar to the Bible – but which is its opposite in its underlying perspective, because *The Laws of Manu* is a spiritual text for those who would *ascend in life.* Nietzsche says that *Manu* is "an incomparable spiritual and superior work; it would be a sin against spirit even to mention its name in the same breath as that of the Bible."[33] He believes that "*The Book of Manu* is *preservative,* whereas Christian morality is *destructive.*"[34]

The Christian construct of the Holy Lie is a philosophy that weakens men and the social unit by breeding admiration of the lesser and abnegation of the higher type. *The Laws of Manu*, on the contrary, neither lowers the higher types nor raises the lower types; they remain at precisely the status they have attained. Thus, to Nietzsche, it has not erected a Holy Lie to disempower men. Instead, it uses a tradition to raise man to a level that corresponds to Nietzsche's ideal society. In "the order of castes," Nietzsche writes, "the highest, the most dominant *Gesetz*, is only the sanction of a natural-order, natural-legal-positing of the first rank, over which no willfulness, no 'modern idea' has power."[35] According to Don Dombowsky,

---

[33]   LUISETTI, F., "Nietzsche's Orientalist Biopolitics" in *BioPolitica* (2011), 6.

[34]   BERKOWITZ, R., "Friedrich Nietzsche, The Code of Manu, and the Art of Legislation," in *New Nietzsche Studies*, Vol. 6-7: 2005-2006.

[35]   BERKOWITZ, "Friedrich Nietzsche, The Code of Manu, and the Art of Legislation."

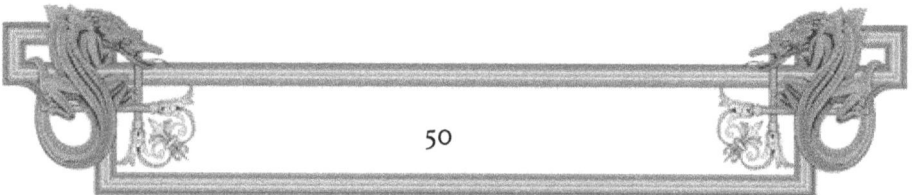

"Nietzsche refers to the law-book of Manu as 'an affirmative Aryan religion, the product of the ruling class.'"[36]

At this point it should be abundantly clear that Nietzsche's political ideas have nothing in common with modern politics at all, and rather shows that he was seeking to completely transcend what is commonly thought of as politics today, thus consigning the entire corpus of Left- and Right-wing ideologies to the dustbin of history. However, his theories of religion will surpass even this revolutionary act, for the death of God also entails a Dionysian resurrection. Nietzsche's study of Hellenic mythology and his theories concerning Christianity eventually lead to his most controversial idea: the symbol of Dionysus and his relation to the Antichrist.

---

[36] DOMBOWSKY, *Nietzsche's Machiavellian Politics*, 61.

DIONYSUS AS ANTICHRIST, HADES AS SATAN

Indeed, my friends, believe with me in this Dionysiac life and in the rebirth of tragedy! Socratic man has run his course; crown your head with ivy, seize the thyrsus, and do not be surprised if tiger and panther lie down and caress your feet! Dare to lead the life of tragic man, and you will be redeemed. It has fallen to your lot to lead the Dionysiac procession out of India to Greece. Gird yourselves for a severe conflict, but have faith in the thaumaturgy of your god![1]

The opposition between Apollo and Dionysus is one of *The Birth of Tragedy*'s core themes. In early works, the synthesis between Apollo and Dionysus described previously is incomplete; they are still two opposing principles: "Thus in *The Birth of Tragedy*, Apollo, the god of light, beauty, and harmony is in opposition to Dionysian drunkenness and chaos."[2] The fraternal union of Apollo and Dionysus that forms the basis of Nietzsche's view is, according to him, symbolized in art, and specifically in Greek tragedy.[3] Greek tragedy, by its fusion of dialogue and chorus, and

[1] GROTTANELLI, C., "Nietzsche and Myth" in *History of Religions* (Chicago: University of Chicago Press, 1997), 3.

[2] PFEFFER, R., *Nietzsche: Disciple of Dionysus* (Cranbury, NJ: Associated University Presses, 1977), 31.

[3] Ibid.

image and music, exhibits for Nietzsche the union of the Apollonian and Dionysian, a union in which Dionysian passion and dithyrambic madness merge with Apollonian measure and lucidity. Chaos and pessimism are overcome in a tragic attitude that is affirmative and heroic.[4]

Neither god can function effectively without the workings of the other. In one there is always an element of the other, for as Nietzsche writes, "There is no Dionysian appearance (*schein*) without an Apollonian reflection (*wierderschein*)." Dionysus appears, thanks to the Apollonian principle, and in return, Dionysus can shroud Apollo in shadows and imperceptible mystery. Apollo communicates to his brethren through the sedate arts. Dionysus whispers the words of seduction and intoxication, whether in the form of theatre, music, altered states of consciousness, or other mediums. As Nietzsche himself says,

> [i]n order to grasp these two tendencies, let us first conceive of them as the separate art-worlds of dreams and drunkenness. These physiological phenomena present a contrast analogous to that existing between the Apollonian and the Dionysian.[5]

Furthermore, Apollo is not just a god of rational clarity and calculated standards; he is also one of boundary-drawing and "of the *principium individuationis*."[6] Apollo therefore represents logic, but also restriction. By contrast, Dionysus expands his horizons by transcending boundaries: hence the Dionysian 'intoxication' "is the

---

[4] Ibid., 51.

[5] NIETZSCHE, F., trans. FADIMAN, C. P., *The Birth of Tragedy* (New York: Dover Publications, 1995), 1.

[6] YOUNG, J., *Nietzsche and the Philosophy of Religion* (Cambridge: Cambridge University Press, 2006), 21.

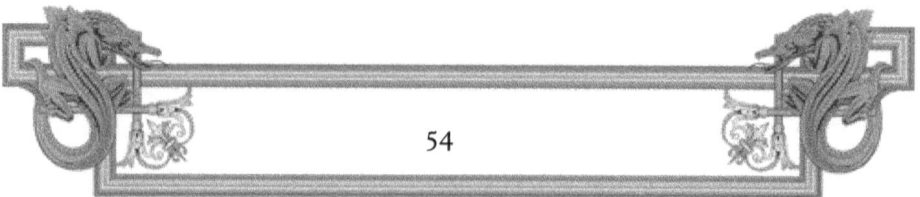

transcendence of the mundane and of all imposed limits."[7] It is when Apollo's influence wanes that the pure essence of Dionysus can be revealed,

> The moment of Dionysian "terror" arrives when [...] a cognitive failure or wandering occurs, when the principle of individuation, which is Apollo's "collapses" [...] and gives way to another perception, to a contradiction of appearances and perhaps even to their defeasibility as such (their "exception"). It occurs "when [one] suddenly loses faith in [...] the cognitive form of phenomena. Just as dreams [...] satisfy profoundly our innermost being, our common [deepest] ground [*der gemeinsame Untergrund*], so too, symmetrically, do "terror" and "blissful" ecstasy [...] well up from the innermost depths [*Grunde*] of man once the strict controls of the Apollonian principle relax. Then "we steal a glimpse into the nature of the Dionysian."[8]

The Apollonian and the Dionysian are dual cognitive states in which art appears as the power of nature in man.[9] For Nietzsche, art is fundamentally not an expression of culture but is instead what Heidegger calls "*eine Gestaltung des Willens zur Macht*": a manifestation of the Will to Power. And since the Will to Power is the essence of being itself, art becomes "*die Gestaltung des Seienden in Ganzen*," a manifestation of being as a whole.[10] This concept of the artist as a creator, and in turn an aspect of the creative process being the manifestation of the will, is a crucial component of Nietzsche's thought: it is the artist, the creator who diligently scribes

---

[7] Ibid.

[8] PORTER, J. I., *The Invention of Dionysus: An Essay on the Birth of Tragedy* (Stanford, CA: Stanford University Press, 2002), 50-51.

[9] Ibid., 221.

[10] Ibid., 205-206.

the new value tables. Taking this into account, we must also accept the possibility that *Thus Spake Zarathustra* opens the doors for a new form of thinker who, rather than working with paint or clay, instead creates the *Übermensch*: the artist who etches his social vision on the canvas of humanity itself. It is in the character of the *Übermensch* that we see the unification of the Dionysian (instinct) and Apollonian (intellect) as the manifestation of the Will to Power, to which Nietzsche also assigns the following tautological pronouncement: "*The Will to Truth is the Will to Power.*"[11] This can be interpreted as meaning that by attributing the will to instinct, truth exists as a naturally occurring phenomenon: it exists independently of the intellect, which allows for many different interpretations of the truth in its primordial state. The truth lies primarily in the will, the subconscious, and the creative potential that Nietzsche identifies with Dionysus. However, Dionysus remains conjoined to his twin, Apollo. Apollo, as the principle of appearance and individuation, is the conscious aspect, which grants form to the hidden Dionysian aspect, without which Dionysus remains bereft of physical appearance:

> That [Dionysus] appears at all with such epic precision and clarity is the work of the dream interpreter, Apollo [...] His appearances are at best instances of "typical 'ideality,'" epiphanies of the "idea" or "idol," mere masks and after images (*Abbilde*[*er*]). To "appear" Dionysus must take on a form.[12]

In his natural state, Dionysus has no form. It is only through his connection to Apollo, who represents the *nature of form*, that Dionysus, as the *nature of the formless*, can appear to us at all. Likewise, Apollo without Dionysus becomes lost in a world of

---

[11] PFEFFER, *Nietzsche*, 114.

[12] PORTER, *The Invention of Dionysus*, 99.

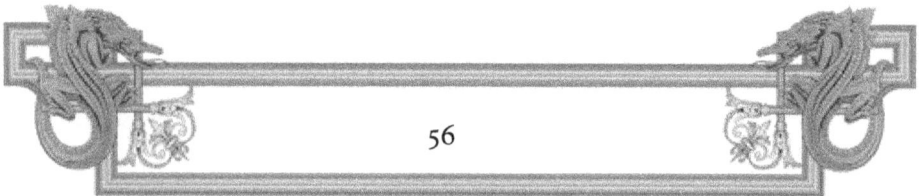

form: the complex levels of abstraction derived from the Dionysian impulse are absent. Neither god can function effectively without the workings of the other. This is Nietzsche's rendition of Apollo and Dionysus, his reworking of the Hellenic mythos, forged into a powerful philosophy that has influenced much of the modern era. Yet how close is this new interpretation to the actual mythology of the ancient Greeks, and how much of this is Nietzsche's creation? To fully understand Nietzsche's retelling of the Dionysus myth and separate the modern ideas from those of the ancients, we need to examine the Hellenic sources.

Apollo is frequently mentioned in connection to Dionysus in Greek myth. Inscriptions dating from the third century BCE mention that Dionysos Kadmeios reigned alongside Apollo over the assembly of the Theben gods.[13] Likewise, on Rhodes, a holiday called *Sminthia* was celebrated in memory of an occasion when mice attacked the vines there and were destroyed by Apollo and Dionysus, who shared the epithet *Sminthios* on the island.[14] They are even cited together in the *Odyssey* (XI 312-25), and also in the story of the death of Koronis, who was shot by Artemis at Apollo's instigation because she had betrayed the god with a mortal lover.[15] The twin peaks on Parnassos are also traditionally known as the "peaks of Apollo and Dionysus."[16] A Pindaric Scholiast says that Python ruled the prophetic tripod on which Dionysus was the first to speak oracles; Apollo then killed the

[13] DETIENNE, M., trans. GOLDHAMMER, A., *Dionysos at Large* (Cambridge, MA: Harvard University Press, 1989), 18.

[14] GERSHENSON, D. E., "Apollo the Wolf-God" in *Journal of Indo-European Studies*, Monograph no. 8, 32.

[15] KERÉNYI, K., *Dionysos: Archetypal Image of Indestructible Life* (Princeton: Princeton University Press, 1976), 103.

[16] POZZI, D. C., & WICKERMAN, J. M., *Myth and the Polis* (Ithaca, NY: Cornell University Press, 1991), 139.

snake and took over.[17] Moreover, their worship was closely entwined at Delphi, for as Leicester Holland has pointed out:

> (1) Dionysus spoke oracles at Delphi before Apollo did; (2) his bones were placed in a basin beside the tripod; (3) the omphalos was his tomb. It is well known, moreover, that Dionysus was second only to Apollo in Delphian and Parnassian worship; Plutarch, in fact, assigns to Dionysus an equal share with Apollo in Delphi.[18]

Myths describing Dionysus separately from Apollo often depict a stranger, an outsider to the community, or represent another culture. Unsavory characteristics that the Greeks tended to ascribe to foreigners are attributed to Dionysus. Various myths depict his initial rejection by the *polis* – yet Dionysus' birth at Thebes, as well as his name's appearance on Linear B tablets, indicates that he is no stranger, but is in fact a native, and that the foreign characteristics ascribed to him are really Greek characteristics.[19] Rather, Dionysus embodies the archetype of an *outsider*: someone who sits outside the boundaries of the cultural norm, or who represents the disruptive element in society which by its nature either effects a change or is removed by the culture which its very presence threatens to alter. As such, Dionysus represents the hidden elements in life itself, which are often dangerous or believed to be impure. As Plutarch observed, Dionysus represents blood, semen, sap, wine, and all the life-giving fluids. This disruptive element is an obvious metaphor for the vital force itself, the hidden essence of life and energy, as a representation of raw nature. This notion of life is intricately interwoven into the

---

[17] FONTENROSE, J., *Python: A Study of Delphic Myth and its Origins* (Berkeley, CA: University of California Press, 1959), 376.

[18] FONTENROSE, *Python*, 375.

[19] POZZI & WICKERMAN, *Myth and the Polis*, 36.

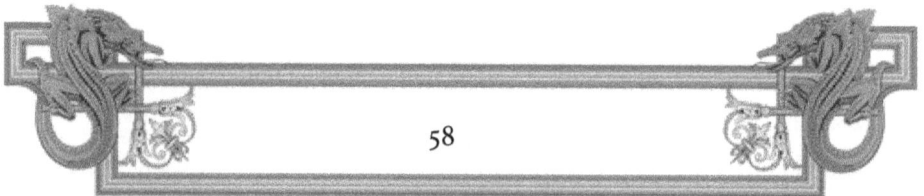

figure of Dionysus in the esoteric understanding of his cult, and indeed throughout the philosophy of the Greeks themselves. The Greeks had two different words for life, both possessing the same root as *vita* (Latin: life), but present in very different phonetic forms: *bios* and *zoë*.[20]

> Plotinus called *zoë* the "time of the soul," during which the soul, in its course of rebirths, moves on from one bios to another [...] the Greeks clung to a not-characterized "life" that underlies every bios and stands in a very different relationship to death than does a "life" that includes death among its characteristics [...] This experience differs from the sum of experiences that constitute the bios, the content of each individual man's written or unwritten biography. The experience of life without characterization – of precisely that life which "resounded" for the Greeks in the word *zoë* – is, on the other hand, indescribable.[21]

Zoë is life in its immortal and transcendent aspect and is thus representative of the pure primordial state. It is a product of life in accordance with a dialectic that is a process not of thought, but of life itself, of the *zoë* in each individual *bios*.[22] There is, therefore, a distinction between mortal, tangible life and another aspect which is immortal and imperceptible to the naked eye. *Zoë*, as the aspect associated with Dionysus, lies beneath the surface, representing the subconscious Chthonic energies that link Dionysus to the Hellenic Underworld. These dark energies can also manifest in other ways, and Dionysus likewise reflects the snake's Chthonic symbolism. The myth of his dismemberment by the Titans tells us that he was born of Persephone, after Zeus (or more likely, Hades) had impregnated her

---

[20]   KERÉNYI, *Dionysos*, xxxxi.

[21]   Ibid., xxxxv.

[22]   Ibid., 204-205.

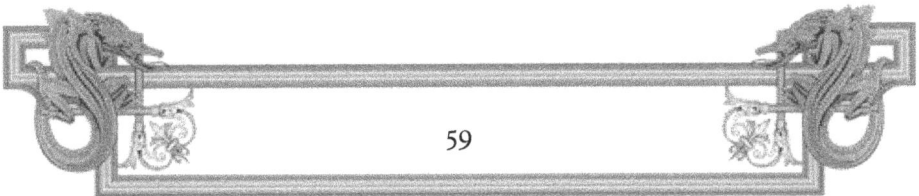

while taking the form of the snake.[23] In Euripides' *Bacchae*, Dionysus, as the son of Semele, is a god of dark and frightening subterranean powers, once again playing the role of a liminal outsider that transits from one domain to another.[24] Because of his connection to natural forces, Dionysus was worshiped in a "temple in the open air, an open-air *naos* with an altar and a cradle of vine branches; a fine lair, always green; and for the initiates a room in which to sing the *evoe*."[25] This stands in direct contrast to Apollo, who was represented by architectural and artificial beauty. Dionsyian music was similarly radically different to that of Apollo's, "for his music is varied, not distant and monotone like the tunes of Apollo's golden lyre."[26]

Both gods are concerned with the imagery of life, art, and as we shall soon see, the sun. Though their forces are entirely opposed, the two gods represent twin polarities of the same force, occasionally meeting in perfect balance to reveal the creative process of life itself and the true esoteric nature of the solar tradition: '*as above, so below.*' Just as Dionysus is a Chthonic deity (*Chthon* meaning Underworld and *Gē* being the physical Earth), Apollo is a solar deity, but not the physical aspect of the sun, which is rather the god Helios. Apollo instead represents the human aspect of the solar path and its application to the mortal realm; rather than being the light of the sky, Apollo is the light of the mind: intellect and creation. In Dionysus the instinct, the subconscious will, and the *zoë* is prevalent, yet nonetheless also has solar connotations. Dionysus rules during Apollo's absence in Hyperborea because the sun has passed to another land; the reign of the bright sun has passed and the reign of the *dark winter sun* is now

---

[23] FONTENROSE, *Python*, 378.

[24] POZZI & WICKERMAN, *Myth and the Polis*, 147.

[25] DETIENNE, *Dionysos at Large* (London: Harvard University Press, 1989), 46.

[26] EURIPIDES, *Bacchae* 126-134 & 155-156, in POZZI & WICKERMAN, *Myth and the Polis*, 144.

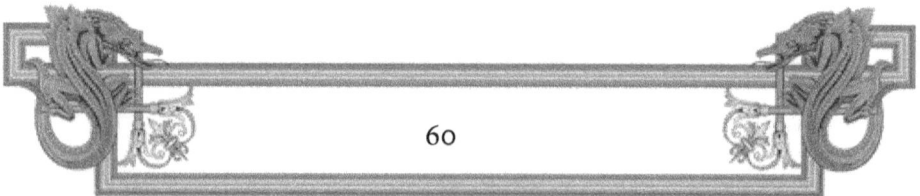

commencing, as represented by Apollo's departure in this myth. This dark sun, associated with rites of the dead and the Underworld, is best described as the Chthonic sun, when it is hidden from one side of the world during winter and at night.

The link between the two occurs not just because of their respective roles in the arts, but because they both have solar connections: one to the sun in the sky, the other to the sun in the Underworld. This relationship is also echoed in the commemoration of the Great Flood, which was celebrated each year at a Delphian festival called *Aiglē*, and took place over two or three days before the full moon in January or February. It occurred simultaneously with the Athenian *Anthesteria* festival, the last day of which was devoted to commemorating the victims of the Great Flood, and at the same time of the year when Apollo is said to return from his sojourn among the Hyperboreans. Moreover, Dionysus is believed to have perished and was resurrected in the Flood.[27]

Apollo's Hyperborean absence symbolizes his annual death. Apollonios says that "Apollo shed tears when he went to the Hyperborean land; thence flows the Eridanos, on whose banks the Heliades wail without cease; and extremely low spirits came over the Argonauts as they sailed that river of amber tears."[28] This departure coincides with Dionysus' reign at Delphi, in which he was the center of worship for the three winter months when Apollo was absent. Plutarch, himself a priest of the Pythian Apollo, an Amphictyonic official, and a frequent visitor to Delphi, says that "for nine months the *paean* was sung in Apollo's honor at sacrifices, but at the beginning of winter the paeans suddenly ceased, then for three months men sang *dithyrambs* and addressed themselves to Dionysus

---

[27] GERSHENSON, "Apollo the Wolf-God," 61.

[28] FONTENROSE, *Python*, 387.

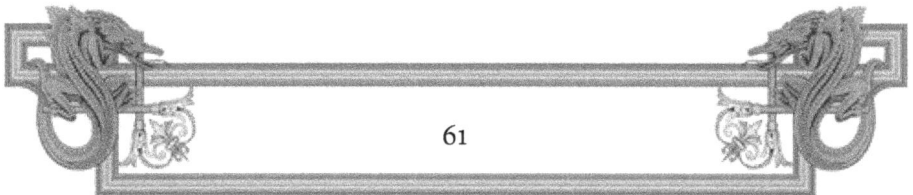

rather than to Apollo."[29] Chthonian Dionysus also manifested during the Athenian Anthesteria winter festival, when the souls of the dead rose to walk briefly in the upper world again, which was the counterpart of the Delphian Theophania. The Theophania marked the end of Dionysus' reign and Apollo's return, after which Dionysus and the ghosts descended once more to Hades' realm.[30] In this supernatural aspect, Dionysus represents not just death, but also eternal afterlife. The *zoë* was employed in Dionysian rites to release "psychosomatic energies, summoned from the depths that were discharged in a physical cult of life."[31] This life persists even during Apollo's absence, for as much as Apollo is the golden sun, Dionysus is the dark winter sun, reigning in the world whilst Apollo's presence departs to another hemisphere.

Far from being antagonistic opposites, Apollo and Dionysus were so closely related in Greek myth that according to Deinarchos, Dionysus was killed and buried at Delphi beside the golden Apollo.[32] Likewise, in Aischylos' *Lykourgos* tetralogy, the cry of "Ivy-Apollo, Bakchios, the soothsayer" is heard when the Thracian bacchantes, the Bassarai, attack Orpheus, the worshiper of Apollo and the sun. The cry suggests a higher knowledge of the connection between Apollo and Dionysus, the dark god, whom Orpheus denies in favor of the luminous god. In Euripides' *Lykymnios*, the same connection is attested by the cry, "Lord, laurel-loving Bakchios, Paean Apollo, player of the Lyre."[33] Similarly, we find another paean by Philodamos addressed to Dionysus from Delphi: "Come hither, Lord Dithyrambos, Bakchios [...] Bromios now in the spring's holy

---

[29] Ibid., 379.

[30] Ibid., 380-381.

[31] Ibid., 219.

[32] Ibid., 388.

[33] Kerényi, *Dionysos*, 233.

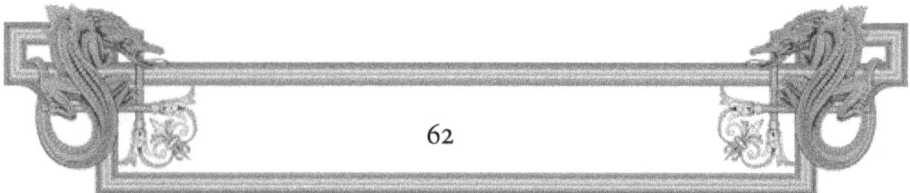

period."[34] The pediments of Apollo's temple also portray Apollo with Leto, Artemis, and the Muses on one face, and on the other Dionysus and the thyiads. A vase painting dating from c. 400 BCE also shows Apollo and Dionysus in Delphi pressing their hands together.[35]

In tandem, Apollo and Dionysus form a *coincidenta oppositorum*. Nietzsche's Dionysus is, therefore, also a reconciler of opposites who absorbs the characteristics of his counterpart Apollo into himself, creating form from his natural state of formlessness, becoming whole when the two merge as one. Kocku von Stuckrad also emphasizes this, writing that "Apollo, it is true, more and more loses his name to the other god, but by no means the power of his artistic creativeness, forever articulating but the Dionysian chaos indistinct shapes, sounds, and images, which are Dionysian only because they are still aglow with the heat of the primeval fire."[36] Not only did Nietzsche comprehend the nature of the opposition between Apollo and Dionysus, he understood this aspect of their cult on the esoteric level: their forces are not antagonistic but complementary, with both gods performing two different aesthetic techniques in the service of the same social function, which reaches its pinnacle of development when both creative processes are elevated in tandem within an individual.

Nietzsche understood the symbolism in the myths and literature concerning the two gods and elaborated upon it, adding Arthur Schopenhauer's ideas to create a complex philosophy concerning not only the interplay of aesthetics in the creative process but also the nature of the will and the psychological process used to create

---

[34] Ibid., 217.

[35] OTTO, W. F., *Dionysus: Myth and Cult* (Dallas: Spring Publications, 1989), 203.

[36] VON STUCKRAD, K., "Utopian Landscapes and Ecstatic Journeys: Friedrich Nietzsche, Hermann Hesse, and Mircea Eliade on the Terror of Modernity" in *NUMEN,* no. 57, 83.

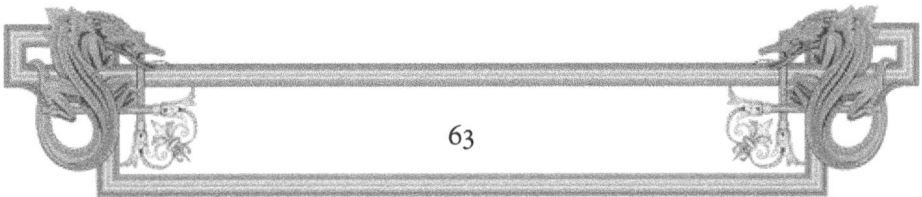

a specific type. This is exemplified in both of his symbols of the ideal: the *Übermensch* and the Free Spirit. Both of these higher types derive their impetus from the Dionysian and Apollonian drives' synchronicity, hence why in Nietzsche's later works following *The Birth of Tragedy* only the Dionysian impulse is referenced, as this term does not signify only Dionysus but rather the balanced integration of the two forces. This ideal of eternal life (*zoë*) is also found in Nietzsche's theory of eternal recurrence. It denies the timeless eternity of a supernatural God, but affirms the eternity of the ever-creating and ever-destroying powers in nature and man, for like the solar symbolism of Apollo and Dionysus, it is a notion of cyclical time. To Nietzsche, the figure of Dionysus is the supreme affirmation of life, the instinct and the Will to Power, with the Will to Power being an expression of the will to life and to truth in their highest exaltation:

> It is a Dionysian Yea-Saying to the world as it is, without deduction, exception, and selection [...] it is the highest attitude that a philosopher can reach; to stand Dionysiacally toward existence: my formula for this is *amor fati*.[37]

Dionysus is thus the highest expression of life in its primordial and transcendent meaning for both Nietzsche and the Greeks: the hidden power of the sun and the subconscious impulse of the will. Dionysus' symbolism has an added layer of complexity, however, which Nietzsche refers to in enigmatic fashion, often with ambiguous sincerity disguised as what could easily be dismissed as a private and deliberately cryptic pun. These unique statements uttered by Nietzsche connect Dionysus not only to Jesus, but also to his adversary, the Antichrist.

---

[37] PFEFFER, R., *Nietzsche*, 261.

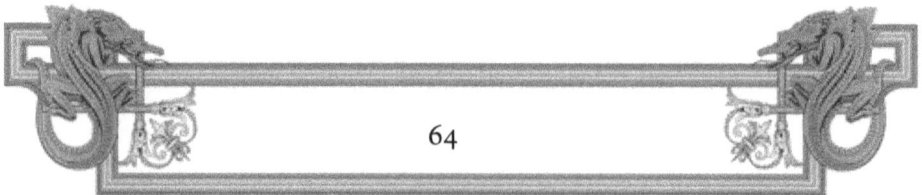

Nietzsche as the Antichrist?

Although Nietzsche changed his stance on many issues throughout his career, some of his core ideas remained constant, including his understanding of Dionysus and Jesus. Even his correspondence bears testimony to his conception of religion and eternal recurrence: eight of his letters bear the signature "Dionysus," while eight others are signed as "the Crucified." Moreover, Nietzsche's comments about the Antichrist harken back to *The Birth of Tragedy*, where he explores the possibility of a counter-teaching to Christianity:

> What was it to be called? As a philologist and man of words I baptized it, not without a certain liberty – for who knows the true name of the Antichrist? By the name of a Greek god: I called it Dionysus.[38]

Nietzsche goes on to later write, "I am a world-historical monster – I am, in Greek, and not only in Greek, the Antichrist."[39] This is the aspect of his writings which has led to profound misunderstanding, namely the opposition that Nietzsche posits between Dionysus and Jesus Christ. While some consider it a wild foreshadowing of Nietzsche's later mental illness, it is equally possible that he was engaging in a very subtle game with his readers. This becomes apparent when Nietzsche, in an allusion to the appearance of Jesus before Pilate, writes: "Have I been understood? – Dionysus versus

---

[38] SHAPIRO, G., *Nietzsche's Earth: Great Events, Great Politics* (Chicago: The University of Chicago Press, 2016), 101.

[39] DOMBOWSKY, D., *Nietzsche's Machiavellian Politics* (New York: Palgrave Macmillan, 2004), 12.

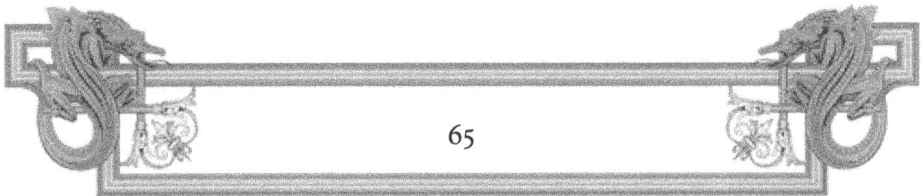

NIETZSCHE: THE ANTICHRIST & THE ANTIPOLITICAL

Crucified."[40] It is not an idle question, and it stands out in the text for precisely this reason. It is important to his philosophy, not because of what he writes but rather because of what he chooses to omit. For Nietzsche, "Dionysus is the name of the Antichrist."[41]

This, again, is drawn from Greek mythology, and concerns Dionysus' paternal ancestry. Dionysus' mother is Persephone (or Semele), and his father is often believed to be Zeus. However, according to Károly Kerényi, it is more likely that Dionysus is the son of Hades, Persephone's husband. Since Persephone is married to Hades, it makes sense that Hades would be his father, not Zeus. Kerényi contends that Hades, not Zeus, is Dionysus' father. This is evinced in his full name: Zeus Katachthonius, or Chthonius, which as Kerényi points out is Hades' title designating him as the sovereign of the Underworld and the royal brother of Zeus. Kerényi explains that

> when mention is made of "another Zeus" or "the hospitable Zeus of the departed," this always refers to Hades. It never means "another god of the daylight heavens," but a ruler of the Underworld who corresponds and is equal to the Zeus of the world above.[42]

Other strong evidence for Hades being the father of Dionysus is cited by Heraclitus of Ephesos, who describes their relationship in an even more precise fashion, plainly stating that "Hades is the same as Dionysus, for whom they rave and act like *bacchantes*." This renders the relation even clearer: Dionysus is not merely the son of Hades, he is an incarnation of Hades that manifests in the world of the living. Kerényi writes that,

---

[40] SHAPIRO, *Nietzsche's Earth*, 1.

[41] Ibid.

[42] KERÉNYI, *The Gods of the Greeks* (London: Thames & Hudson, 1961), 230.

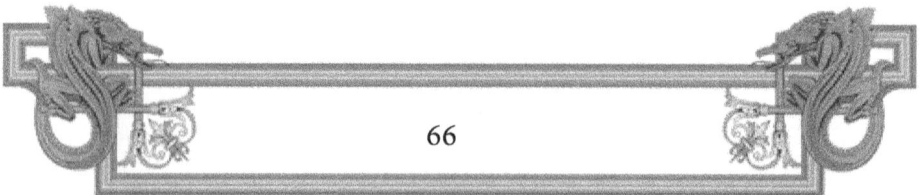

[f]or Heraclitus, this identity was a crucial fact, which he could invoke because it was known to all. He used it in support of his own philosophy of the identity of opposites, and because of his philosophy, he was able to recognize and express, as could no one else, the importance of the unity of the god Dionysus and Hades.[43]

Walter Otto also places great emphasis on this statement by Heraclitus, and prefers to adhere to this explanation over modern interpretations of Dionysus:

This god, he says, is the same god as Hades. What can keep us from believing him? Is it his practice to indulge in arbitrary interpretations? His aphorisms, however paradoxically they may sound, bear witness to the nature of things. Should what he saw in Dionysus mean nothing to us? Consider, too, how much he must have known about the Dionysus of the sixth century, which is lost to us today. Consequently, his comments must stand as one of the most important bits of evidence that have down to us. We can now understand why the dead were honored at several of the chief festivals of Dionysus.[44]

Otto also links Hades to Dionysus by citing line 330 of Aristophanes' *Frogs*, which lists the myrtle as one of Dionysus' favorite plants. Dionysus gave the myrtle to Hades, at Hades' request, as a surrogate for Semele, which is the basis of the belief that the myrtle belonged both to Dionysus and to the dead.[45] And this is not the only evidence to suggest that Hades and Dionysus are not simply related but are different aspects of the same god.

---

[43] KERÉNYI, *Dionysos*, 240.

[44] OTTO, *Dionysus*, 116.

[45] Ibid., 158.

Surviving relics also support this understanding, such as a *calyx-krater* which depicts the god Poseidon and his relationship to Dionysus. In the composition, Poseidon looks across to an enthroned god distinguished by a long scepter, situated in the same low region, and three serving figures before him also point at him: an Eros and two nobly-dressed Dionysian women standing on either side of a large *krater*, with one woman holding a wine pitcher that is probably empty. The other god resembles Poseidon, and is clearly not lower in rank; evidently, he is the ruler of the Underworld, Hades, and Dionysus in one – Poseidon's brother.[46]

Nietzsche also refers to a female figure from Greek myth: Ariadne, the partner of Dionysus. Ariadne is the bride of Dionysus, but she is also linked to Persephone, the wife of Hades. The name Ariadne, originally "meant 'holy' and 'pure,' and was a superlative form of Hagne, a surname of the Queen of the Underworld."[47] In the myths in which Dionysus is born from Semele, he is still connected to Persephone, for the *Pseudo-Hyginus* (Fabulae 167) states that it is Persephone who gives the heart of Dionysus Zagreus to Semele in a drink, which impregnates her with Dionysus' second incarnation. This heavily implies that Dionysus is not only a form of Hades, but that Ariadne is also a form of Persephone. However, they are manifestations which inhabit the world of mortals, and not the purely Chthonic forms which remain in the Underworld. Nietzsche even mentions the name Ariadne in connection with females to whom he was attracted, which serves to illustrate just how deep his self-identification with Dionysus was.

This unexpected intrusion of the Greek god of the dead might be more surprising than the usual appearances Dionysus makes in Nietzsche's writings. However, it is necessary to explain this to

---

[46] KERÉNYI, *Dionysos*, 297.

[47] KERÉNYI, *The Gods of the Greeks*, 269.

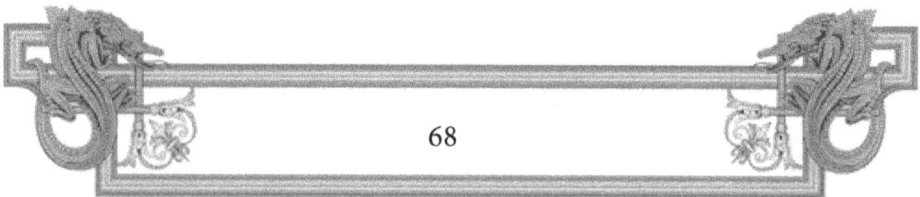

understand his references to both Dionysus and the Antichrist – including Nietzsche's letters, where he referred to himself as the Antichrist, and where he wrote about 'Dionysus vs. the Crucified.' If we accept the evidence that Dionysus is another aspect of Hades, and that Nietzsche, being exceptionally well-versed in Greek mythology and an admirer of Heraclitus (who stated that Dionysus was Hades), then we must interpret this as meaning 'Hades (Dionysus) vs. God (the Crucified),' which posits a much stronger adversary and a much darker image of Nietzsche's 'Antichrist.' Though Nietzsche may have been joking when he signed his letters in this bizarre fashion, the connection between Hades and the Christian 'Hell' is no laughing matter.

Hades rules as King in the Chthonic world of the dead, having taken on this role at the end of the Titanomachy, when the Titans were imprisoned in Tartarus. The Underworld is therefore not Hades' creation; it is rather bequeathed to Hades after he and his brothers divide power, with Hades reigning as the equivalent of Zeus himself in the Underworld.[48] Whilst there is no equivalent of Hell (except for Tartarus, a separate area of the Underworld) in Greek mythology, certain aspects of Hades did indeed inspire the creation of the Christian Hell, which did not exist in the earlier Jewish tradition.[49]

The original term for the equivalent to the Underworld in Christianity, Hell, is derived from the Greek realm of Hades, which in turn is not equivalent to the modern conception of Hell but rather with that of the Hebrew Sheol. Christian mythology interprets Hell to be purely a place of punishment, which is not the case in either the Greek Hades or the Hebrew Sheol, which is where all mortals

---

[48] HARASTA, J. & CHARLES RIVER EDITORS, *Hades: The History, Origins and Evolution of the Greek God* (Scotts Valley, CA: CreateSpace, 2013).

[49] Even the current Pope has admitted that Hell does not exist, indicting that even the Vatican is aware of the historical precedent for Hell.

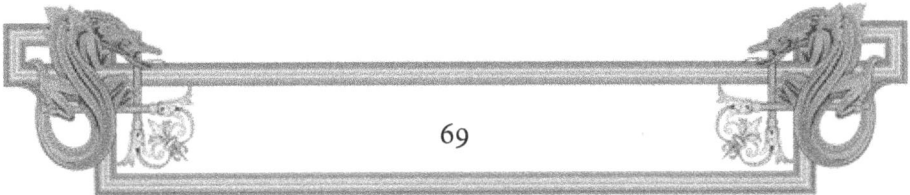

who have not won the dram of immortality which allows them to ascend to the heavens with the immortals spend the afterlife in their respective traditions. Thus, Hades and Sheol are not purely for 'sinners,' but are the domiciles of the ordinary dead. The bleak emptiness of parts of Hades can also be immediately contrasted with the afterlife found in the Elysian Fields and on the Isles of the Blest,[50] emphasizing that it was not all punishment and sorrow in the world below.

Sheol, which came to be mistranslated as Hell, simply means a grave or death[51] in its original Hebrew context. In the Old Testament, the word Sheol occurs sixty-four times, out of which it is translated three times as 'pit,' twenty-nine times as 'grave,' and thirty-two times as 'Hell.'[52] This illustrates how the meaning of the word shifted from the original Hebrew one to a purely Christian conception. There are four words in the original languages of the Bible which are all translated as Hell in the common English version: Sheol, Hades, Tartarus, and Gehenna.[53] Sheol and Hades simply translate as grave or as an afterlife in the Underworld; only Tartarus and Gehenna correlate with the Christian Hell as a place of punishment.[54] Balfour, quoting Campbell, further elaborates on the origin of the word Hades and how it came to be associated with the Christian Hell:

> As to the word Hades, which occurs in eleven places of the New Testament, and is rendered Hell in all, except one, where it is translated grave, it is common in classical authors and frequently

---

[50] KERÉNYI, *The Gods of the Greeks*, 248.

[51] BALFOUR W., *An Inquiry into the Scriptural Import of the Words Sheol, Hades, Tartarus, and Gehenna* (London: Forgotten Books, 2016), 20.

[52] Ibid., 9.

[53] Ibid., 2.

[54] Ibid., 7.

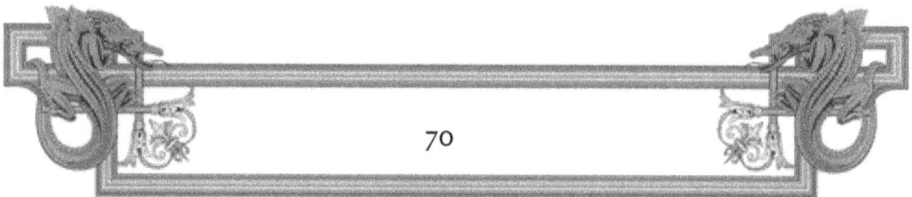

used in the translation of the Old Testament. In my judgment, it ought never in Scripture to be rendered Hell, at least in the sense wherein that word is universally understood by Christians. In the Old Testament, the corresponding word is Sheol, which signifies the state of the dead in general, without regard to the goodness or badness of the persons, their happiness or misery. […] This word is also used sometimes in rendering the nearly synonymous words or phrases *bor* and *abre bor*, the pit, and stones of the pit, *tsal moth*, the shades of death, *dumeh*, silence. This state is always represented under those figures which suggest something dreadful, dark and silent, about which the most prying eye, and listening ear, can acquire no information. The term Hades, is well adapted to express this idea.[55]

The Greek Chthonic Kingdom of Hades and the Sheol of the Jews were conflated, eventually becoming the biblical Hell we are familiar with in the West. It also raises many philosophical and soteriological issues for those of the Christian faith, the implications of which are outside of the scope of this book, however. Suffice to say that if Hades and Hell are in fact based on the same portrayal of an after-life in the Chthonic world, then the King of Hades and the ruler of Hell are the same entity – making the figure of the biblical Satan closely identified in Christian thinking with the Greek god Hades, and by default, Dionysus.

The transformation of Hades occurred before the god was conflated with the mythical Satan, and primarily originated with the confusion of the Hebrew *Sheol* with the Greek *Hades*. In the case of Hades, however, the transformative process is a different one, which juxtaposes the role of death with that of judging the souls of the dead – and incorporating many different deities from rival polytheistic traditions into the single entity popularly known as 'Satan,' which is

---

55   Ibid., 3-4.

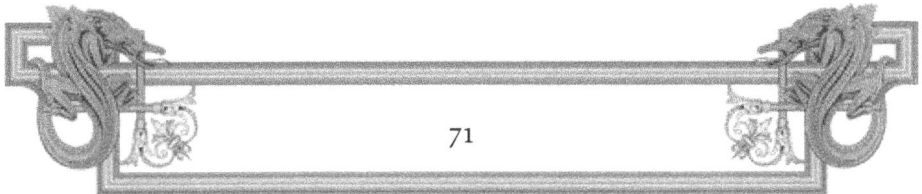

actually simply a word for 'adversary', and, moreover, the name given to quite literally *all* adversaries of Middle Eastern monotheism. This is not to say that Hades and Satan are the same entity, for *an entity named Satan never existed at all*, and it was merely a title derived from the word *Shaitan*, meaning 'adversary.' Thus, in many early Christian depictions of Hell, both Satan and Hades are named as the rulers of Hell.

The interesting thing about this, however, is that if Dionysus is the son of or an incarnation of Hades, and Hades is associated with Satan, then Dionysus literally becomes the figure of the Antichrist that Nietzsche writes of. When Nietzsche asks his famous question, "Dionysus versus the Crucified, am I understood?," the answer can only be an affirmative one – but not in the sense of Dionysus being evil in the Christian context. Rather he is a god of both life and death, as Hades reborn into the world of the living. As Otto says,

> [t]he madness which is called Dionysus is no sickness, no debility, but a companion of life at its healthiest. It is the tumult which erupts from its innermost recesses when they mature and force their way to the surface. It is the madness inherent in the womb of the mother. This attends all moments of creation, constantly changes ordered existence into chaos, and ushers in primal salvation and primal pain – and in both, the primal wildness of being. For this reason Dionysus, in spite of his association with the spirits of the underworld, with the Erinyes, Sphinx, and Hades, is a great god, a true god; that is, the unity and totality of an infinitely varied world which encompasses everything that lives.[56]

Dionysus therefore has a robust connection to the Christian concept of the Antichrist via Hellenic accounts, and also as a

---

[56] OTTO, *Dionysus*, 143.

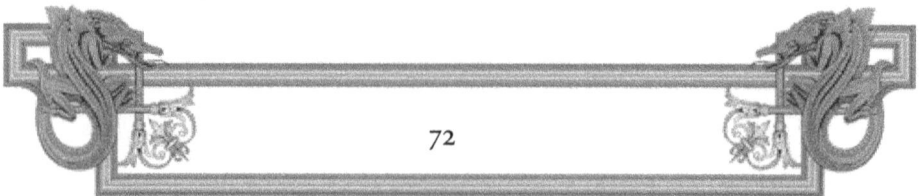

result of mistranslations of both Hebrew and Greek texts by early Christian scholars. The Antichrist, rather than being a departure from Nietzsche's previous work on Dionysus, is an extension of it, which reaches its full expression in the publication of *Der Antichrist*. This connection is primarily revealed through the writings of one of Nietzsche's primary inspirations, the Greek philosopher Heraclitus, who openly states that Dionysus and Hades are the same gods, with Hades being the father of Dionysus (not Zeus). Hades is one of the main deities combined into the composite adversary of Christianity, 'Satan,' via a convoluted process involving numerous mistranslations of Hebrew terms.

Nietzsche appears to have understood that Dionysus and the Antichrist are essentially the same entity, and strongly implied that Christianity is no longer aware of its real origins: 'Satan' was never a single entity, but rather an adversary created from rival polytheistic faiths of the same era. This aspect of Nietzsche's thinking has been disappointingly obfuscated by Nietzsche's cleverness, leaving philosophers and academics unable to understand his subtle puns about the Antichrist, perhaps as a final private joke. As Nietzsche himself would say, "He who laughs best today will also laugh last."

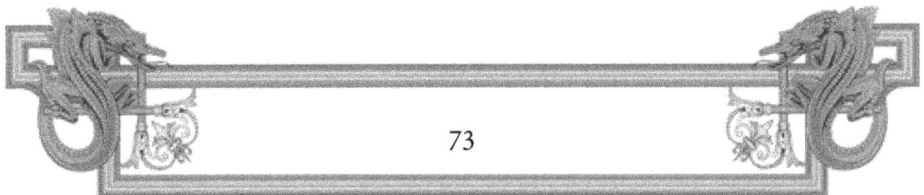

THE ANTIPOLITICAL
NIETZSCHE

THE PHYSICIAN OF CULTURE

ietzsche wrote a letter to Erwin Rohde during March 1873 telling him that he was thinking of naming the book he was writing – a book that he never completed – *The Philosopher as the Physician of Culture*. There can be little doubt that Nietzsche believed his work would heal some of the ailments afflicting Western culture. On the surface, Nietzsche's work is often deeply critical of both religion and politics, so the cultural intentions of his philosophy are not always immediately perceptible. Nonetheless, Nietzsche intended to have an effect that would drastically alter the nature of civilization, hence his conception of the philosopher as a 'physician of culture.'

The comparison of the city/polis with the human body has been a theme in philosophy since the time of Plato, as explained earlier. It can be understood as a biological analogy relating the body's organs working together as a single organism, mirrored on a larger scale in society as a whole, which is viewed as a body in itself. This idea can also be found in non-Western cultures, such as in the *varṇas* or castes of Hinduism. This metaphor, however, has another layer of interpretation: physiology was still a very new science during Nietzsche's lifetime, and his choice of terminology thus reflects an interest in the science of his day. Accordingly, when Nietzsche speaks of himself as the 'physician of culture,' society is the organism that he intends to cure. N. Martin describes the importance of the 'healing' function in Nietzsche's philosophy below:

> Since physiology and the body ('*Leib*') play a major part in Nietzsche's diagnosis of the European illness, Nietzsche as a physician tries to create conditions that would make a new strengthening of will and will-power possible. [...] As a physician, Nietzsche is concerned with the 'normal' health of humankind and peoples, and with the means of strengthening will-power so as to regain capacity to say a 'Dionysian yes' to the world 'as it is.'[1]

Culture provides a mechanism for common interests and objectives that can tie a civilization together. The pre-modern methods of unifying a nation were different than they are today; people could easily be united through shared ethnicity, tradition, and religion. In the contemporary West, however, this cohesion no longer exists. Modern democracies often host multiple ethnicities, tradition has been replaced by legislative procedure, and religion has been abandoned almost entirely in some nations. Under such conditions, culture is the most viable tool with which to cultivate national sentiment and communal pride.

The idea of culture as a defining characteristic of the nation is not unique to Nietzsche. It is also found in the views of Johann Gottfried von Herder, who proposed that there was a "popular spirit" or *Volksgeist* at the core of nationalism.[2] What neither Herder nor Nietzsche expected, however, was that the West's cultural

---

[1] MARTIN, N., *Nietzsche and the German Tradition* (Oxford: Peter Lang, 2003), 244.

[2] BIRNS, N., "Ressentiment and Counter-Ressentiment: Nietzsche, Scheler, and the Reaction Against Equality," in *Nietzsche Circle*, www.nietzschecircle.com/RessentimentMaster.pdf, 15.

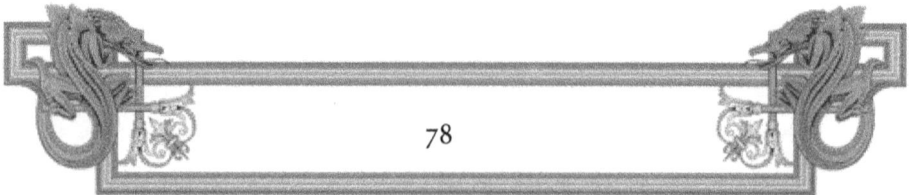

production would soon be severely impaired by the rise of a heavily mass production-based 'worker' society. This mass production/worker society is a hybrid of both capitalism and socialism. It has its roots in the revolt of the bourgeoisie, as Nicholas Birns relates: "The valorization of labor, originally upheld by the bourgeoisie as a reaction to the disinterested and therefore "unproductive" nobility, provided the first substitute for identity."[3] As a consequence of this modern democracies, by embracing capitalism and the 'valorization of the worker', have created a nation that is no longer capable of generating authentic culture. The necessity for both men and women to work full-time in a society driven by mass production requires that in order to achieve even basic subsistence, the time involved in pursuing culture, as well the cultivation of interest in culture, are severely curtailed. Achievements in the arts, humanities, or other areas that create cultural values are likewise denigrated to such an extent that even tradesmen are held in higher esteem. Those who do pursue cultural achievements typically profit little from their endeavors. The final result of this is that creative efforts are left stillborn, the ramifications of which, though subtle today, will one day become deadly as modern society fractures into several opposing groups, none of which will profess loyalty to the unifying community, nation, or civilization. By abandoning the cultural aspects of the State, the heart of a culture corrodes, and entropy spreads slowly to poison the entire political system. This leaves the modern nation with a very real conundrum: what constitutes national identity in a modern society where tradition and religion have been displaced? And furthermore, can it even be achieved without those who once created culture, such as artists and humanities scholars?

Birns also raises this question when he states that while "contemporary 'nationalism' might well be founded on a political ideal of State and citizenship, it would nevertheless be a mistake to

---

[3] Ibid., 20.

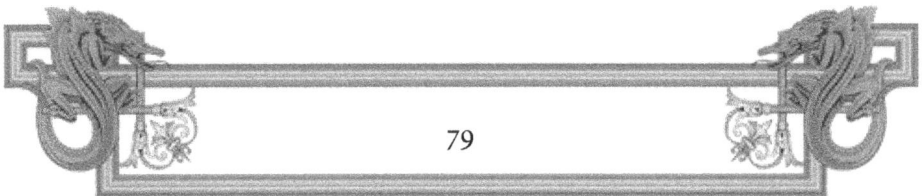

believe that abstract political values are sufficient to create a common identity, and especially that they would suffice to convince their members to accept the sacrifices they sometimes require."[4] Even the very liberal John Stuart Mill wrote that democracy cannot function in a pluralistic society, saying that "[d]emocratic power belongs to the people, but only if the people are united."[5]

Nietzsche himself likewise espouses this sentiment in *The Birth of Tragedy*, where he describes culture as the "most basic foundation of the life of a people."[6] The modern nation-state, however, has become increasingly complex, and the more it grows, the weaker its ties to the people and the original concept of State becomes. Familiarity is essential in creating communal bonds, but the very size of the modern State renders this difficult. This leads to the development of micro-communities which ultimately serve to destabilize the social structure. This is not only bad for the nation, but also for those who govern the State, because it creates a distinction between "us" and "them," and this perceived disparity dissolves the foundation of collective identity necessary for a national culture. As such, the elected representatives of modern democracies immediately find themselves in opposition to a large group of disgruntled citizens who have no real loyalty to the State, and are instead controlled purely by legislation and coercive force alone. In the worst-case scenario, this leads to both *ressentiment* and revolution.

Ressentiment is the mother of all revolutions, and all political authorities should be wary when the chasm between the powerful and the powerless yawns dangerously wide. One solution to this problem is to resolve such conflicts through State coercion. This was not Nietzsche's desire, however. Far from endorsing oppressive

---

[4] Ibid., 22.

[5] Ibid., 12.

[6] STRONG, "Nietzsche and the Political," 48.

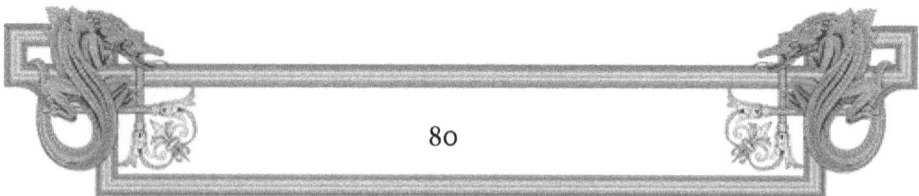

regimes, Micheal Ure informs us that Nietzsche "shares with the Hellenistic schools the belief that the central motivation for philosophizing is the urgency of human suffering and that the goal of philosophy is human flourishing, or *eudaimonia*."[7] However, "in the early 1880s Nietzsche took a stand against the Stoic goal of removing the emotions from human life – against the idea that *eudaimonia* turns on the achievement of *apatheia*,"[8] which will eventually become Nietzsche's classic prescription for happiness: *amor fati* – to love one's fate, regardless of what it entails.

Fate, however, decrees that nothing lasts forever. Empires and nations will always rise and fall. There is no man-made social structure that can last forever, and our current one is no exception. But once an idea or concept successfully survives the ravages of history long enough to become venerable, it passes into tradition and myth – thus making them not mere superstitions, but instead the enduring and most robust feature of any cultural or ancestral heritage. Cristiano Grottanelli believes that "every culture that has lost myth has lost, by the same token, its natural, healthy creativity."[9] And when a culture loses its creative power, it begins to die. Myth is a link to a shared tradition and community, and when it is present, the State is more vital and healthier. According to Ure, this is what Nietzsche means when he is[r]eferring to himself as "the physician of culture," Nietzsche's ambition is to prescribe for the State the medicine which he believes will cause culture to flourish and make the State healthy once again, by utilizing culture as the stimuli for what Heidegger will later call "Being." In becoming a "physician of culture," Nietzsche also reveals his own influences that served to

---

[7] URE, M., "Nietzsche's Free Spirit Trilogy and Stoic Therapy" in *The Journal of Nietzsche Studies*, no. 38 (2009), 62.

[8] Ibid., 72.

[9] GROTTANELLI, C., "Nietzsche and Myth" in *History of Religions* (Chicago: University of Chicago Press, August 1997), 2.

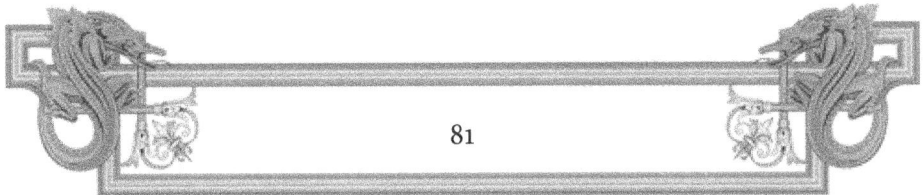

create his "Being," which are largely derivative of his own knowledge of Hellenic philosophy and culture, for "Like all the Hellenistic philosophers, Nietzsche seems to have arrived at the view that the source of our misery is not to be found in things but in the value judgments that we bring to bear upon things and we can be cured of our ills only through a change in our value judgments."[10]

Nietzsche argues that this displacement of the value of life is the symptom of an illness that he refers to as *décadence*,[11] and it is not only tied to *ressentiment*, but also to cultural erosion. The man who proselytizes *ressentiment* for political or religious reasons does so because of *décadence* – he cannot rise to power via honest, honorable methods, so due to his weakness he has to control the strong by other means. It is a debasement of the Will to Power, which is still found in weaker types, who deploy it against society in order to control others. For Nietzsche, this is the sickness and corruption rampant in modern society:

> In both *Beyond Good and Evil* and, earlier, in *The Gay Science*, Nietzsche uses "corruption" (Corruption, *Verfall, Verderb*) as a term indicating the general stage of decline in the life cycle. Weakness of the will, then, the diagnosis of modern man's particular affliction, is one of many possible forms this corruption might have taken, since "corruption (Corruption) is something totally different depending on the organism in which it appears."[12]

Nietzsche's vision for society therefore relies on improving culture, but the means by which he wishes to enact this is not necessarily political, or at least not political in the sense in which most people

---

[10] URE, "Nietzsche's Free Spirit Trilogy and Stoic Therapy," 72.

[11] SCHOTTEN, C. H., *Nietzsche's Revolution: Décadence, Politics, and Sexuality* (New York: Palgrave Macmillan, 2009), 4.

[12] Ibid., 46.

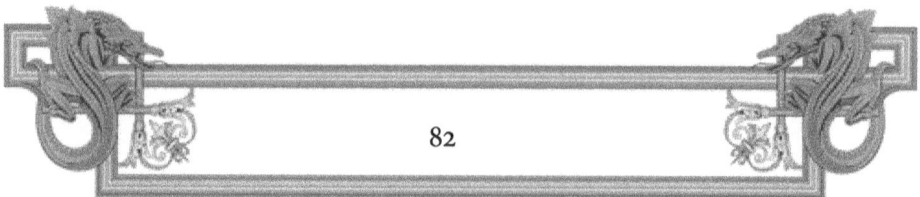

understand the term. Nor can Nietzsche strictly be classified as apolitical, for despite the fact that he states that he is antipolitical, "he means he is antistatist and pro-cultural, but he may also mean, more specifically, that he is antisocialist and antidemocratic in conformity with a convention in German conservative political philosophy."[13] This statement has to be interpreted in the context of his own era rather than our own, in which the term antipolitical takes on a meaning closer to being apolitical. Antipolitical, in contrast to apolitical, means that Nietzsche was *against* the political system, and not merely ignoring it. Again, this indicates that he did not believe that the notion of the State was the way forward for Europe, but rather that the purpose of the state "should be 'a nobler form of humanity' and it should regard itself only as a 'means' to this end."[14] The term antipolitical also has another meaning for Nietzsche:

> According to Peter Bregmann, the term anti-political emerged during the religious wars when the Politiques defended the new notion of the secular commonwealth by labeling anti-political all those who insisted on a theocratic conception of politics. Thomas Paine, in the eighteenth century, would denounce Edmund Burke's defense of church and State as "anti-political." In the late nineteenth century, the term was adopted by political scientists, similarly seeking to protect the political from new threats to its autonomy.[15]

This does not imply that Nietzsche had an interest in a theocracy, however, for he is definitely not in favor of any form of Christian rule. However, it does strongly suggest that Nietzsche adopted this

---

[13]   DOMBOWSKY, D., *Nietzsche's Machiavellian Politics* (New York: Palgrave Macmillan, 2004), 106-107.

[14]   Ibid., 107.

[15]   DETWILER, B., *Nietzsche and the Politics of Aristocratic Radicalism* (Chicago: University of Chicago, 1990), 59.

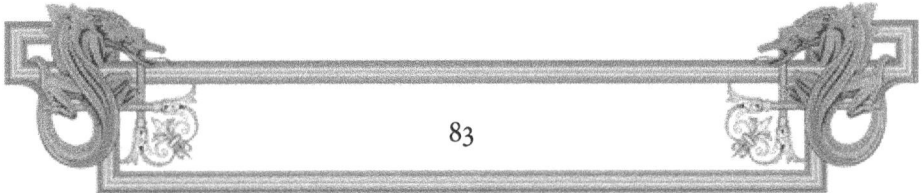

term in a heretical sense, to defy the dominion of the State over his work and writing, and that he believed in maintaining a certain respectable distance between politics and philosophy. In general Nietzsche viewed these as incompatible: "For he who has the *furor philosophicus* within him will already no longer have time for the *furor politicus*, and will wisely refrain from reading the newspapers every day, let alone working for a political party."[16] Given the political decline that would occur in Germany after his death, Nietzsche was very prudent in taking measures to distance himself from political propaganda and the media.

Being antipolitical does not necessarily entail completely disengaging from politics, but rather those forms which ultimately become 'unhealthy' and decadent. The duty of the true philosopher is to create remedies for the maladies which beset society, and the solution is to devise a better system of politics, since "all subduing and becoming master involves a fresh interpretation."[17] It is with this in mind that Nietzsche espouses *aristocratic radicalism* and its ancillary strategy of *große politik*, which is to be implemented at an ideological and cultural level via a war he termed the *Geisterkrieg*.

---

[16] Ibid.

[17] SCHOTTEN, *Nietzsche's Revolution*, 75.

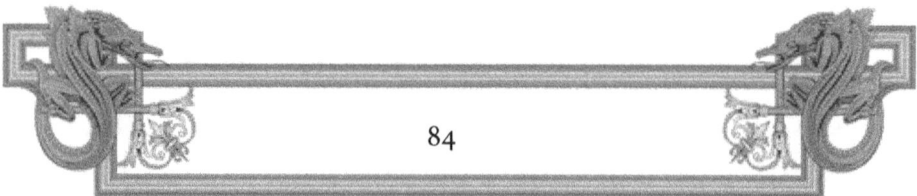

THE ANTIPOLITICAL NIETZSCHE

There can be no doubt that Nietzsche is still one of the most misunderstood philosophers of all time, partly due to his literary style and changing opinions over the course of his career. The other problem is that because his ideas are deliberately obfuscated by his penchant for using metaphors and making cryptic comments, readers are left with a sense of vagueness and are tempted to 'flesh out the details' with their own – potentially mistaken – ideas. This is most prevalent in the area of politics. Though Nietzsche, as we have seen in the previous chapters, clearly did have ideas which could be implemented politically on the cultural and religious levels, as a 'physician of culture' Nietzsche posited himself as being quite firmly outside of the realm of everyday politics. Nevertheless, he still sought to influence it by alternating the subliminal flow of the narrative that runs in the deep substrata of civilization upon which politics rests, like a form of erosion in which water, after hundreds of years, carves through solid rock. The question therefore remains: if a Nietzschean *Übermensch* ever succeeds in overthrowing the current political system, what remains to govern the people? The idea Nietzsche actually purposes is radically different from both aristocracy and democracy; indeed, it is well and truly outside of most people's comprehension.

The era in which Nietzsche lived was undergoing a political transition and upheaval as empires and monarchies gradually gave way to democracy and nation-states. Although National Socialism and fascism did not exist until several decades after Nietzsche's death, the debate as to whether or not he provided some of the philosophical background for these movements continues. This is painfully ironic considering how much Nietzsche despised the political currents of his day which eventually culminated in National Socialism, as well as other political organizations. This debate is ill-founded for two reasons in particular.

Firstly, it is important to note that Nietzsche provides his own definition of race, which is different from the biological understanding of the term used today. Nietzsche defines it as "peoples living for a longer time in a specific environment ('*Umgebung*') and developing a '*Charakter*' of their own in such environments."[1] For him, race is closer to culture and further from biology or physiognomy. When Nietzsche does use the term '*Rasse*' (race), "in most instances, it means 'people' ('*Volk*') [...] 'social classes' ('*Stände*'); and it can also refer to human beings in general ('*Mensch*,' '*Menschheit*,' '*Menschentyp*')."[2]

Secondly, Nietzsche was openly hostile to the political powers of his era, as L. P. Thiele relates:

Indeed, Nietzsche intentionally made his published work politically obnoxious lest his public role as a writer constitute an infraction of this edict: "I write in such a way that neither the

---

[1] MARTIN, N., *Nietzsche and the German Tradition* (Oxford: Peter Lang, 2003), 237.

[2] Ibid., 238.

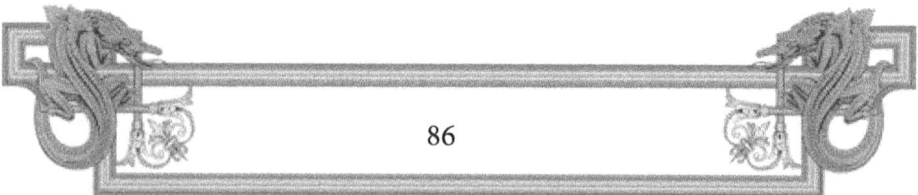

mob, nor the *populi*, nor the parties of any kind want to read me [...] Neither usefully nor pleasantly – to the trio I have named."[3]

Despite this, Nietzsche has continued to wield a posthumous influence over politics, although in many cases he has either been deliberately misappropriated or simply misunderstood. Even in our own time, we need only look at America, where the so-called founders of the Alt-Right fantasized about being *Übermenschen* whilst embodying *chandala* traits. These terrible interpretations of Nietzsche amount to precisely what he was opposed to: the appropriation of his work for distasteful political phantasmagoria.

The German National Socialists were the most notorious movement to appropriate Nietzsche's work for political purposes. Nietzsche's abhorrence of Wagner's antisemitism shows what he would have thought of Adolf Hitler however. Nevertheless, such ideas were commonplace in Germany during Nietzsche's lifetime. Indeed, Nietzsche's own sister, Elisabeth, who outlived her brother by four decades, later became a prominent supporter of National Socialism, and the National Socialists themselves cherry-picked his writings to make it seem as if he had been a prophet of their ideology. As a consequence, despite the fact that an objective appraisal of Nietzsche's ideas shows how far he actually was from National Socialism, his legacy is still condemned to be haunted by its specter.

Many of the political ideas we take for granted in the twenty-first century either did not exist or were only just beginning to develop during Nietzsche's lifetime. Thus, Nietzsche's political views must be interpreted in this historical environment. Modern democracy was still a recent innovation, following many centuries of aristocratic reign over Europe. Monarchical forms of government were still the norm. As a result, it was natural for many people to be skeptical

---

[3] THIELE, L. P., *Friedrich Nietzsche and the Politics of the Soul: A Study of Heroic Individualism* (Princeton: Princeton University Press, 1990), 47.

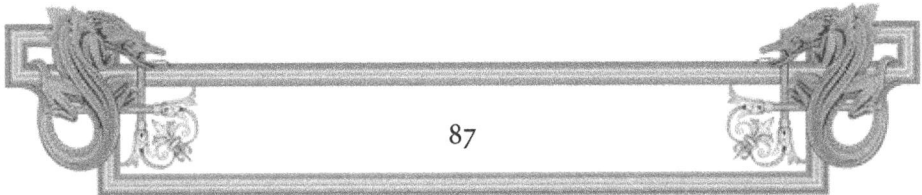

of democratic trends. Nietzsche's correspondence suggests that between 1858 and 1868, he "held essentially conventional political views that corresponded entirely to the conservative program of national liberalism in Germany."[4]

Democracy was not the only new political innovation in Germany. Racial theories, drawing upon the work of Joseph Arthur de Gobineau began to appear, along with new scientific theories such as Charles Darwin's notion of evolution. Nietzsche was sometimes critical of Darwin, despite his negative opinion of Christianity and its own efforts to oppose evolution. Nietzsche's critique of Darwinism is mainly rooted in his idea that human beings strive solely for power, "which implies that a struggle for existence or a will to life was the fundamental human drive [and] is one from which he feels the need to distinguish himself."[5]

Thus, the advent of democracy, Darwin, and de Gobineau set trends in motion which culminated in a veritable tempest of political unrest. Darwin's theories led to the development of selective breeding and euthanasia programs, and were soon connected to the emerging theories on race, along with a mythos of 'Aryan' conquest fueled by British colonialist misinterpretations of Indian history. All of this ultimately combined in the National Socialist movement. National Socialist ideology was created out of erroneous indology research, the theory of race, Social Darwinism, and skepticism regarding democracy, all of which were mainstream currents at the time. As Christian J. Emden succinctly explains, "The racist doctrines of nineteenth-century anthropology and archaeology started as unsophisticated prejudices that could easily be refuted, but by the

---

[4]   EMDEN, C. J., *Friedrich Nietzsche and the Politics of History* (Cambridge: Cambridge University Press, 2010), 39.

[5]   SORGNER, S. L., "Nietzsche, the Overhuman, and Transhumanism" in *Journal of Evolution and Technology*, vol. 20, no. 1 (2009), 29-42.

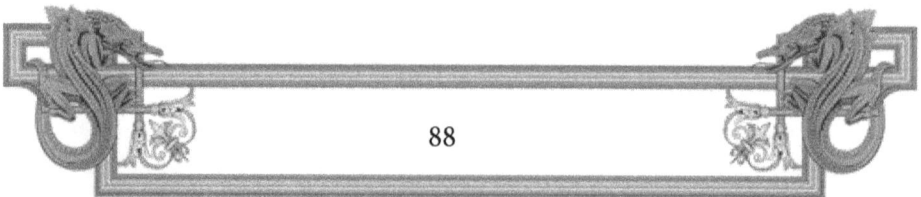

end of the century they had become intellectualized to such an extent that even liberal-minded anthropologists and archaeologists began to subscribe to them."[6]

Outside of Germany, Nietzsche's influence in politics predated the advent of fascism in Italy when his books attracted the attention of the poet Gabriele D'Annunzio. D'Annunzio introduced Nietzsche's work to a wider audience in Italy, describing his works as a way to prepare for "its use in an aristocratic key."[7] The rebellion against modernization, the need for an aristocracy of intellectuals (which D'Annunzio saw himself as leading), as well as the cult of strength and strong anti-democratic biases were all prominent themes in his writings.[8] Unlike Nietzsche, though, D'Annunzio actively engaged with politics.[9] Thus, Nietzsche's ideas found a place in Italian politics earlier than they did in Germany.

Italian fascism is also incompatible with Nietzsche's philosophy, for several reasons. For one, Nietzsche adamantly opposed the nationalist belief in a "folk-soul" and thought it was a "basic error" to think of "collective" wills.[10] Therefore, rather than calling for a German superpower, Nietzsche instead called for the unification of Europe and for a "new caste" to dominate it, which he termed the "Good European."[11] This "Good European represents an

---

[6] EMDEN, *Friedrich Nietzsche and the Politics of History*, 187.

[7] SZNAJDER., M., "Nietzsche and Mussolini" in *Nietzsche, Godfather of Fascism: On the Uses and Abuses of Philosophy*, eds. GOLOMB, J. & WISTRICH, R. S. (Princeton: Princeton University Press, 2002), 239.

[8] Ibid., 241.

[9] Ibid., 242.

[10] BUCCOLA, N., "The Tyranny of the Least and the Dumbest: Nietzsche's Critique of Socialism" in *Quarterly Journal of Ideology* , vol. 31, no. 3 & 4 (2009), 27.

[11] HALFERTY DROCHON, H., "The Time Is Coming When We Will Relearn Politics" in *The Journal of Nietzsche Studies*, no. 39 (2010), 71.

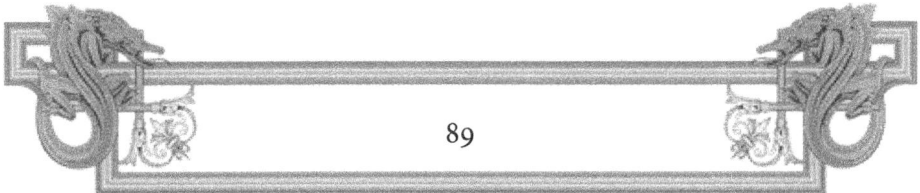

'amalgamation of nations' and the 'mutual blending and fertilization' of cultures.'[12] Dombowsky relates that as "early as *Human, All Too Human* (1878–80), Nietzsche says that the 'great task' of the 'Good Europeans' will be 'the direction and supervision of the total culture of the earth.'"[13] Likewise, Nietzsche holds that the State should be used to generate culture, and its "purpose should be 'a nobler form of humanity,' and that it should regard itself only as a 'means' to this end."[14]

Gary Shapiro tells us that Nietzsche "rejects the nation-state, a place that would claim its inhabitants by a parental model of natality, for the sake of a new people and new earth, called his "children's land, yet undiscovered in the most distant sea."[15] This strongly implies that Nietzsche's preferred audience is not a country, nor even a nation, but a group of individuals who set forth to discover their role in the world. This, along with the concept of the Good European, could tie in with claims that certain aspects of Nietzsche's thought are related to geophilosophy.

According to Gilles Deleuze and Félix Guattari, geophilosophy recognizes that thinking does not proceed between subject and object, but rather "takes place in the relationship of territory and the earth."[16] It, therefore, ties man to the ultimate national symbol: the landscape which surrounds them. Herman W. Siemens and Shapiro further argue that "Nietzsche's thought undermines

---

[12] DOMBOWSKY, D., *Nietzsche's Machiavellian Politics* (New York: Palgrave Macmillan, 2004), 109-110.

[13] Ibid., 112.

[14] Ibid., 107.

[15] SHAPIRO, G., *Nietzsche's Earth: Great Events, Great Politics* (Chicago: University of Chicago Press, 2016), 80.

[16] SIEMENS, H. W., "Nietzsche's Critique of Democracy (1870–1886)" in *The Journal of Nietzsche Studies*, no. 38 (2009), 11.

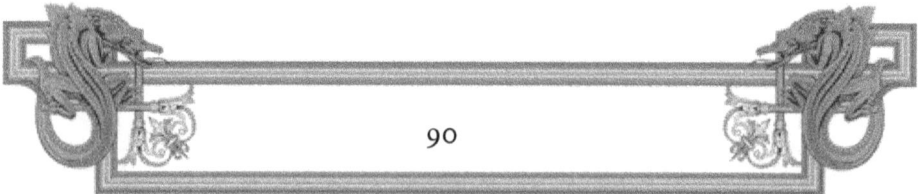

ideologically driven metanarratives of globalization, such as Eduard von Hartmann's *Weltprozess* story, repeatedly ridiculed by Nietzsche, and also the more topical 'end of history' story popularized by Fukuyama."[17] Haroon Sheikh expands on the idea of geophilosophy by connecting geography directly to culture, stating that "the competitive advantage of a country is grounded in its traditional culture."[18] Likewise, "Nietzsche's 'Peoples and Fatherlands [...] locates philosophy in a dynamic tension between deterritorialization (as in philosophy's universalistic claims) and reterritorialization (as in the unavoidable, if largely unconscious reinscription of thought within spatial coordinates)."[19] Deleuze and Guattari also perceive Nietzsche's notion of the "'untimely' (*unzeitmässig*) – as in *Untimely Meditations* – to involve the opening of a geographic rather than a historical perspective."[20] This paves the way for a spatial developmental theory of philosophy instead of a temporal one. However, the temporal manifestation is present in the idea of eternal recurrence: everything repeats save that which is constant, such as the Earth, which offers a 'firm foundation' for philosophy, compared to the fickle whims of history, which is one of the reasons for 'untimely' ideas.

---

[17] SIEMENS, H. & SHAPIRO, G., "What Does Nietzsche Mean for Contemporary Politics and Political Thought?" in *The Journal of Nietzsche Studies*, no. 35/36 (2008), 4.

[18] SHEIKH, H., "Nietzsche and the Neoconservatives: Fukuyama's Reply to the Last Man" in *The Journal of Nietzsche Studies*, no. 35/36 (2008), 41.

[19] SIEMENS & SHAPIRO, "What Does Nietzsche Mean for Contemporary Politics and Political Thought?," 4.

[20] SIEMENS, "Nietzsche's Critique of Democracy," 9.

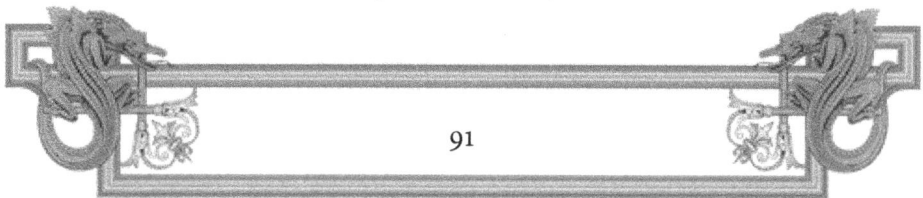

Democracy

Democracy is regarded as something which is above criticism today. But in Nietzsche's time, it was an untested political system, and as such he was wary of it. Given that Germany eventually elevated Hitler to power through democratic means, Nietzsche's suspicions appear well-founded: the people elected a politician who did not benefit their country in the slightest and who caused the deaths of millions, both Jewish and European.

According to Don Dombowsky, Nietzsche's main critique of democracy was based on the belief that democracy was

> '[t]he declining form of the power to organize' and 'the decaying form of the state' – he counts the German Reich as one of its 'imperfect manifestations' – but he will add, following the aristocratic liberal critique, that it is also 'a form of the decay of man, making him mediocre and lowering his value.'[21]

Nietzsche also believed that democracy, like any other political form, can deteriorate, become corrupted, and create a tyranny of the multitude against the individual to the point where "all parties are now required to flatter the 'people' and to give it all kinds of reliefs and freedoms, whereby it finally becomes omnipotent."[22] Again, this transition from democracy to tyranny is best illustrated by Hitler's ascent via the Weimar German democratic system. As such, Nietzsche perceived a much darker undercurrent in democracy in opposition to the modern reverence for democracy. What Nietzsche

---

[21] DOMBOWSKY, *Nietzsche's Machiavellian Politics*, 58.

[22] SIEMENS, "Nietzsche's Critique of Democracy," 25.

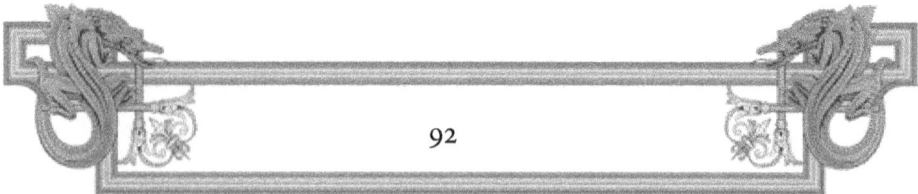

foresaw was how democracy could lead to the loss of freedom by promoting ideas for the masses at the expense of minorities and individuals. Today, people assume this could not occur, yet even a cursory glance at social media reveals how easy it is for politicians to manipulate others into blind obedience by preying on their hopes and fears – or, as Nietzsche would call it, by cultivating political *ressentiment*. It is in this context that one should examine the following statement:

> While the democratization of Europe leads to the production of a type that is prepared for slavery in the subtlest sense, in single, exceptional cases the strong human being will have to turn out stronger and richer than perhaps ever before [...] I meant to say: the democratization of Europe is at the same time an involuntary arrangement for the cultivation of tyrants – taking the word in every sense, including the most spiritual.[23]

In other words, democracy, despite theoretically empowering everyone, simultaneously places actual power in the hands of the few, leaving the system vulnerable for a true tyrant to take over. The only difference is that if such a tyrant emerges in a democracy, then it is ultimately the fault of those who voted for him, and the electorate is as morally culpable as the tyrant. Plato also acknowledged this, understanding how democracy could act as a precursor for tyranny. After all, if the vast majority of citizens are equal but powerless save for a vote, they can easily be dominated by those with more money, resources, and status.

In a democracy, one must also rely on the majority to make good, rational choices – but this assumption may not always be correct. The public can be misled by lies, rhetoric, or can simply make

---

[23] DETWILER, B., *Nietzsche and the Politics of Aristocratic Radicalism* (Chicago: University of Chicago Press, 1990), 175.

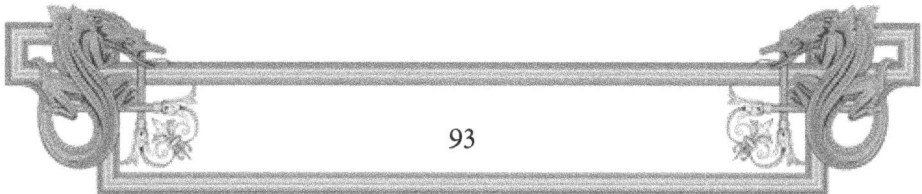

uninformed decisions. The fact that a large number of people believe something in no way implies that such a belief is true. Truth, unlike politicians, is not dependent on popularity. It is this that scares Nietzsche about democracy: people as a mass are capable of making disastrous and catastrophic political mistakes. What Nietzsche feared was the prospect that democracy could create a violent, unthinking mob. If this occurred, a large number of people could adopt a cruel or blatantly incorrect idea that is overtly destructive or harmful to others. In this scenario, as Siemens relates, Nietzsche asks that when

> [g]overnment becomes "but a function of the one and only sovereign, the people," does democracy not run the risk of replacing one kind of tyranny – the tyranny of the despotic genius – with another: the tyranny of the people?[24]

Another problem with democracy that Nietzsche highlights is, as Siemens again points out, that a "hatred of authority is endemic to democracy," which he elaborates as being the "democratic idiosyncrasy against everything that rules and wants to rule, the modern Misarchism (to coin a bad word for a bad state of affairs)."[25] The problem is that there always needs to be some form of hierarchy within any organization for it to function well. No one wants a bad leader, but what about a good leader? Nietzsche's theory of Misarchism implies that one would be despised simply for being in a position of authority, irrespective of whether one's leadership is beneficial or not. This concern of Nietzsche's should again be examined in the context of his particular time, which justifies Nietzsche's wariness of his political environment. Siemens points out that

---

[24] SIEMENS, "Nietzsche's Critique of Democracy," 25.

[25] Ibid., 28.

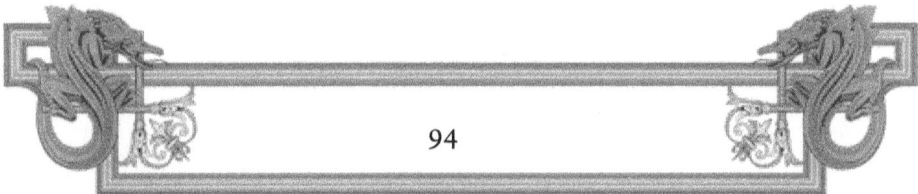

[t]he figure of genius, recast as the deviant, nonconformist, or exceptional human beings (*Ausnahme-Menschen*), looks increasingly fragile and vulnerable to Nietzsche. His emancipatory impulse is detached from the tyranny of genius and transforms into a concern with protecting exceptional individuals from the mob. This much is clear from the texts on misarchism discussed above and from many others from this period. A typical example is note 26[89]: "Exceptional spirits go wrong more easily; the story of their suffering, their illnesses, their rage at the loud quacking about virtue among all the moral ganders, etc. Everything conspires against them, they are embittered at always being out of place. – Danger in democratic ages. Absolute contempt as security measure."[26]

Since Nietzsche was both an intellectual and an outsider, there is an element of self-preservation at work, as well as a genuine interest in protecting other individualists from persecution by the masses. Nietzsche perceives himself as one who is differentiated from the masses, and as such views himself as someone who is outside of mainstream society, observing the Herd from a respectable distance. Nonetheless, he is aware that stampedes can occur, and many a man has met his end under bovine hooves. A such, Nietzsche is positing that his higher type will necessarily be an outsider in some regard, and that in certain specific environments, even those who are slightly different can become a target for mass persecution. In this light, Nietzsche can be seen as one who wishes to save the few from the tyranny of the many.

This element of social differentiation also relates to politics and the mass media, for, as Nietzsche writes, "I am opposed to [...] parliamentary government and the press, because these are the

---

[26] Ibid., 29.

means by which the Herd animal becomes the master."[27] What he means is that the mainstream media is designed to appeal to the average reader and not the intellectuals; thus what is promoted is not necessarily the best, but simply the most popular viewpoint. In this regard, Nietzsche does not see European democracy as a strong or vital system, referring to it as "a release of laziness, of weariness, of weakness."[28] This is also why Nietzsche connects democracy with mediocrity: the vote is controlled by the majority and not by those who are the best informed. Furthermore, when speaking of government, Nietzsche writes that "they know: *mediocritas* is also *aurea*"[29] – meaning that *mediocrity* is *gold*. Additionally, in regard to the party system, he believes them all to be fundamentally untrustworthy: "How treacherous all parties are! They bring to light something about their leaders, which the latter have perhaps always taken great care to hide under a bushel."[30] In a note from 1885, Nietzsche even goes so far as to jest that "[w]e probably support the development and maturing of democratic institutions: they enhance weakness of will."[31]

By contrast, Leo Strauss and Francis Fukuyama have taken another view on culture in regards to Nietzsche's concept of the Last Man, and have sought to interpret Nietzsche in terms of the classical tradition of political theory, in contrast to the "modern political theory that sought to banish the concept of *thymos* from political thought."[32] *Thymos* is a part of the soul mentioned by Plato which

---

[27] NIETZSCHE, F., *The Will to Power*, ed. KAUFMANN, W. (New York: Vintage Books, 1968), 397.

[28] Ibid., 399.

[29] Ibid., 461.

[30] NIETZSCHE, *The Will to Power*, 398.

[31] DETWILER, *Nietzsche and the Politics of Aristocratic Radicalism*, 173.

[32] SHEIKH, "Nietzsche and the Neoconservatives," 29.

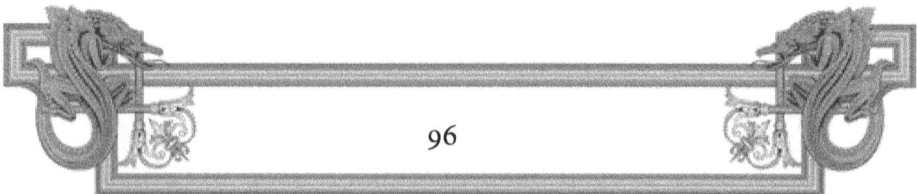

deals with the human drive for recognition and honor. Fukuyama, in particular, interprets Nietzsche's theories that culminate in the idea of the Last Man as a description of *thymos'* decline in the modern world.[33] This highlights the connection between Nietzsche and Hellenic ideas yet again.

Sheikh also contends that Fukuyama agrees with Nietzsche's view regarding the decline of *thymos*, writing that "[d]ue to the end of struggle and the pacification of man, the powerful and violent types like Caesar and Alexander but also the great creative types – artists and writers such as Homer, Michelangelo, or Pascal – can no longer come into existence."[34] However, their links to the world of tradition remain, because

> [t]he modern economy is driven by motives other than the purely material pursuit of comfort. In new forms, ancient authorities still command respect and motivate people, infusing the modern world with traditional *thymos*. Moreover, Fukuyama argues, these are not simple remnants of the past set to disappear in the future but, instead, critically underpin the modern world because they determine, for instance, the success societies have in terms of innovation and economies of scale.[35]

Nietzsche's criticism of politics is what one would expect from a philosopher who had adopted an openly antipolitical stance. His opinions encompass more than his skepticism of newly-emergent modern democracy, however. Socialism and anarchism were also targets of Nietzsche's criticism. Thus, though Nietzsche is antipolitical, this should not be interpreted as anarchism.

---

[33] Ibid.

[34] Ibid., 35.

[35] Ibid., 42.

ON ANARCHY & SOCIALISM

losely related to Nietzsche's critique of democracy are his even more scathing remarks concerning socialism. Indeed, in *The Antichrist* Nietzsche writes: "Whom do I hate most among the rabble today? The socialist rabble...".[1] The term 'socialist rabble' does not mean the voters or the people; this comment is directed at the 'rabble-rousers' (political agitators) who cultivate *ressentiment* in the collective. The socialist, then, seems to be saying,

> I am wretched because 'the system' has made me so! If we overturn 'the system' and punish those who supported it, I will cease to be wretched.[2]

Moreover, as Dombowsky states, Nietzsche equates the socialist conception of society with the "lowest in the order of rank."[3] In other words, socialism, like other forms of *ressentiment*, is a manifestation of the Will to Power in the "least and dumbest members of society."[4]

---

[1] BUCCOLA, N., "The Tyranny of the Least and the Dumbest: Nietzsche's Critique of Socialism" in *Quarterly Journal of Ideology*, vol. 31, no. 3 & 4 (2009), 2.

[2] Ibid., 19.

[3] DOMBOWSKY, D., *Nietzsche's Machiavellian Politics* (New York: Palgrave Macmillan, 2004), 43.

[4] BUCCOLA, "The Tyranny of the Least and the Dumbest," 15.

Effectively the socialist cultivates *ressentiment* in the same manner as the Christians toppled Rome: socialism creates a 'slave revolt' which then proceeds to the cultivation of mediocrity that empowers a democracy.

Nietzsche also links Christian values to the decline of the political climate in the modern West, because to Nietzsche's thinking, Christianity offers the "poor and lowly" a "gateway to happiness," and "to this extent the rise of Christianity is nothing more than the typical socialist doctrine."[5] Indeed, he also believes socialists use Christian ideas for their own purposes: "The socialists appeal to the Christian instincts; that is their most subtle piece of shrewdness."[6] In *The Antichrist*, Nietzsche calls the "equality of souls before God" the "pretext for the rancor of all base-minded, this explosion of a concept which eventually became revolution, modern idea, and the principle of decline of the whole order of society."[7] Socialism is, therefore, a means of agitation employed by individuals in order to attain something; it has to organize into a group to gain power.

Moreover, according to Dombowsky, "Nietzsche views the anarchist, democratic, and socialist movements as the successors of the Christian movement, as neo-Christian and, accordingly, the militant European worker or proletariat, as an avatar of Christian 'anarchist agitation in the Empire."[8] As such, they are very much connected to the slave revolt hypothesis, for as Nietzsche says, "the preaching of altruistic morality in the service of individual egoism is one of the most common lies of the nineteenth century."[9] The target

---

[5] Ibid., 7.

[6] Ibid.

[7] Ibid., 8.

[8] DOMBOWSKY, *Nietzsche's Machiavellian Politics*, 12.

[9] BUCCOLA, "The Tyranny of the Least and the Dumbest," 25.

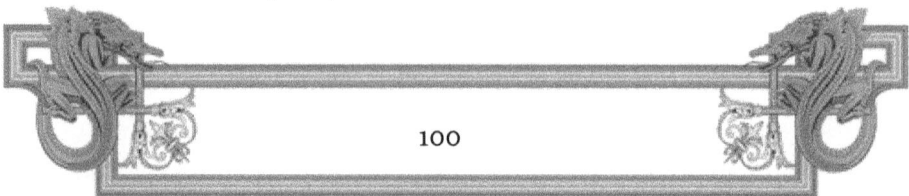

demographic of *ressentiment* can thus be any group which is envied by others within the same cultural grouping. Their villain is "the 'good man' of the other morality, precisely the noble, powerful man, the ruler, but dyed in another color, interpreted in another fashion, seen in another way by the venomous eye of *ressentiment*."[10] Thus, in Nietzsche's slave revolt theory, the group that identifies as oppressed will always be the one that enacts the most brutal vengeance – thus the successful political agitators will always seek to cultivate *ressentiment* in the lowest members of society and promise them both equality and revenge:

> [The underprivileged] need an appearance of justice, i.e., a theory through which they can shift responsibility for their existence, for being thus and thus, on to some sort of scapegoat. This scapegoat can be God – in Russia there is no lack of atheists from *ressentiment* – or the social order, or education and training, or the Jews, or the nobility, or those who have turned out well in any way.[11]

Though Nietzsche also expresses similar disdain for the anarchists, his relationship with anarchism has proven to be much more complex and somewhat contradictory due to some of his comments regarding it. This incongruity occurs because some authors – notably Peter Bergmann – have noticed that Nietzsche's position "most closely resembles that of the anarchists."[12] This similarity arises from a form of individual whom Nietzsche refers to as the *free spirit*. This type of person is akin to the better-known example of the *Übermensch*. However, it is also apparent in Nietzsche's works that the two, although comparable, are not identical. This is made

---

[10]   Ibid., 20.

[11]   Ibid.

[12]   DOMBOWSKY, *Nietzsche's Machiavellian Politics*, 1.

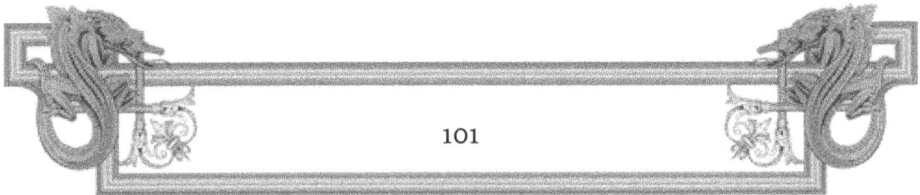

adamantly clear by the fact that Nietzsche uses the two different titles to demarcate the boundary betwixt the two types, thus rendering their respective character traits as similar but distinct. Nietzsche's use of the term 'free spirit' suggests that while these figures may well be a type of anarchist, Nietzsche himself is not endorsing anarchism as a political ideology. Dombowsky, however, suggests that the free spirit should not be interpreted in the following manner:

> The mission of the free spirits is to prepare a reversal of values. Nietzsche describes them as transgressive and expedient, but they do have political ideals. They represent both resistance and recodification in terms of laws, contracts, and institutions, a revaluation which intends to constitute the power of order of rank, and not mere aristocratic democracy or meritocracy in opposition to leveling mediocrity.[13]

What the free spirits are connected to is not anarchism, but aristocracy – or more correctly, *Nietzsche's conception of aristocracy*, which is very different from the form of aristocracy we already know. It is a new aristocracy that Nietzsche speaks of, not the preservation of the old form, which is nigh inseparable from the monarchy. Moreover, these free spirits, despite their anarchistic elements, do play a part in Nietzsche's aristocracy, as Bruce Detwiler demonstrates:

> In a *Nachlass* passage from 1887 that was revised in 1888, Nietzsche clearly identifies the superman as a "higher type" that constitutes the "higher aristocracy" of the future. In other passages, the "new aristocracy" of the future is mentioned interchangeably with "the legislators of the future," the "free spirits" of the future is mentioned interchangeably with "the future masters of the earth," who are in turn mentioned interchangeably with "the legislators

---

13   Ibid., 41.

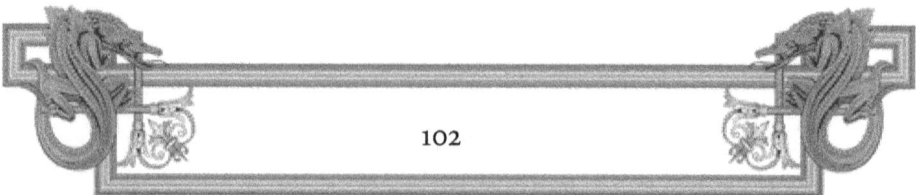

of the future," the "free spirits" of the future, the coming "master race," and the coming "ruling caste," thereby suggesting that all of these terms and phrases are more or less synonymous in his view.[14]

Given these negative views on socialism and democracy in general, one has to pause to consider the enduring popularity of Nietzsche's work in contemporary culture and indeed, one will find plenty of apologists who either try to bypass Nietzsche's political ideas entirely or deliberately try to interpret his ideas in terms of agreement with present-day liberalism. Some authors have gone beyond Nietzsche's ideas and successfully re-crafted them, and in this light there are some noteworthy figures who warrant a separate study, but they fall outside the scope of this book. However, even a cursory glance at Nietzsche's texts reveals that his ideas are not those of any of today's political systems. He is not endorsing socialism, fascism, liberalism, democracy, or even traditional aristocracy. Rather, Nietzsche's political thought is an extension of his work on the Will to Power.

Returning to the political elements of Nietzsche's hypothesis, Nietzsche believes the Will to Power is scorned and denigrated in the modern era because of democratic values. The doctrine of equality reduces everyone to the same faceless substance, and those who express any form of individualization become a potential victim of the Herd's wrath. In such a regime, the Will to Power when it manifests is feared by the Herd. Under these conditions, politics will favor those who are average in order to reduce the threat of change entering into what is otherwise a closed system of thought. As Nietzsche expressed it,

---

[14] DETWILER, B., *Nietzsche and the Politics of Aristocratic Radicalism* (Chicago: University of Chicago Press, 1990), 100.

[o]ur virtues are conditioned, are demanded by our weakness [...] equality, a certain actual rendering similar of which the theory of 'equal rights' is only the expression, belongs essentially to decline: the chasm between man and man, class and class, the multiplicity of types, the will to be oneself, to be standing out – that which I call *pathos of distance* – characterizes every strong age. The tension, the range between the extremes is today growing less and less – the extremes are themselves finally obliterated to the point of similarity.[15]

The point here is that a weak government is likely to be more vicious towards a strong opponent if its ideas run contrary to its own. Thus, excessive doctrines of equality act as a vessel for an insidious form of inequality, by punishing that which dares to think differently and by inherently restricting intelligence and creativity, as well as by removing any true individuation out of fear of the Will to Power:

The Herd feels the exception, whether it be below it or above it, as something opposed and harmful to it. [...] fear ceases in the middle: here one is never alone; here there is little room for misunderstanding; here there is equality; here one's own form of being is not felt as reproach but as the right form of being; here contentment rules. Mistrust is felt toward the exceptions; to be an exception is experienced as guilt.[16]

Furthermore, the power of the Herd is dominant, and the more one is closer to the average citizen in the Herd, the less of an individual nature they possess:

---

[15] JENKINS, M., *Aristocratic Radicalism or Anarchy? An Examination of Nietzsche's Doctrine of Will to Power*, Fellowship Dissertation for the International Society for Philosophers, 20-21.

[16] NIETZSCHE, F., *The Will to Power*, ed. KAUFMANN, W. (New York: Vintage Books, 1968), 159.

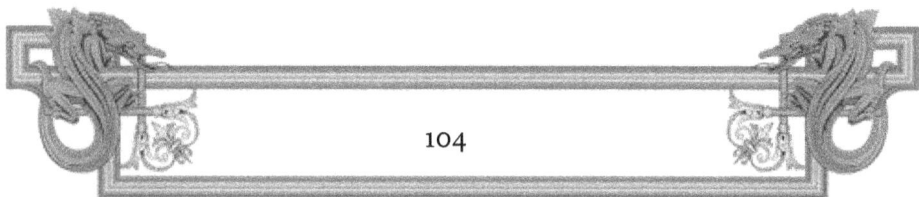

The herd instinct, then – a power that has now become sovereign – is something totally different from the instinct in an aristocratic society; and the value of the units determines the significance of the sum. Our entire sociology simply does not know any other instinct than that of the Herd, i.e., that of the sum of zeros – where every zero has "equal rights," where it is virtuous to be zero.[17]

Nietzsche also purposes that the Herd is opposed to what he defines as an aristocratic society, and that they lessen the Will to Power by conveying the supposition that within the Herd one should seek safety in the mainstream and that those who stray from it are in danger. However, the Will to Power should not be confused with hubris or narcissistic megalomania. Rather, Nietzsche makes it clear that the Will to Power is, in fact, the Will to Life – but some people will always have a greater hunger to experience life, as Nietzsche indicates: "The great and small struggle always revolves around superiority, around growth and expansion, around power – in accordance with the Will to Power which is the Will of Life."[18] Life, as a consequence, reveals its presence in human society via a complex interplay of different strengths and motivations as humans compete for dominance, with the will of the strong conquering and subduing weaker opponents.

In this regard, Nietzsche can be seen to be adhering to Thomas Hobbes' notion of the *bellum omnium contra omnes*. However, like Baruch Spinoza, Nietzsche believes that the State never really emerges from the state of nature.[19] Seen from this angle, society takes on a distinctly Darwinian turn, with intra-species rather

---

[17] NIETZSCHE, *The Will to Power*, 33.

[18] SCHOTTEN, C. H., *Nietzsche's Revolution: Décadence, Politics, and Sexuality* (New York: Palgrave Macmillan, 2009), 32.

[19] DOMBOWSKY, *Nietzsche's Machiavllian Politics*, 32.

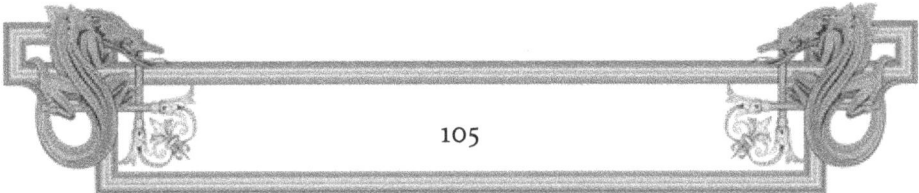

than inter-species competition occurring, as lies at the core of the theory of evolution. Nietzsche, as mentioned earlier, disagrees with Darwin and believes that the Will to Power is the basic human drive underlying life itself. According to Stefan Lorenz Sorgner, for Nietzsche the pursuit of the "Will to Life as the fundamental human drive is one from which he feels the need to distinguish himself."[20] Therefore, the will – either to power or to life – is the method by which one becomes an individual by achieving something that differentiates oneself from the bulk of humanity.

As a consequence, the Will to Power is something that can manifest in many different guises. Like the *Übermensch* and Dionysus, it is an integral part of all Nietzsche's work, and is something he considers to be both healthy and virtuous. Its absence, as well as the fear of individuals who possess it, are the hallmarks of slave morality, and are symptoms of a culture in decline. This is why Nietzsche describes his contemporaries as "men, not noble enough to see the abysmally different order of rank, chasm of rank, between man and man – such men have so far held sway over the fate of Europe, with their 'equal before God,' until finally a smaller, almost ridiculous type, a herd animal, something eager to please, sickly, and mediocre has been bred, the European of today."[21] This epidemic of destructive mediocrity is something Nietzsche also links to the rise of the finance industry and liberalism:

> The power of the middle is, further, upheld by trade, above all trade in money: the instinct of great financiers against everything extreme. [...] They need occasionally to arouse fear of other

[20] SORGNER, S. L., "Nietzsche, the Overhuman, and Transhumanism" in *Journal of Evolution and Technology*, vol. 20, no. 1 (2009), 29-42.

[21] HÖRNQVIST, M., "The Few and the Many: Machiavelli, Tocqueville, and Nietzsche on Authority and Equality," www.italianacademy.columbia.edu/sites/default/files/papers/Mikael%20Hornqvist.pdf, 9.

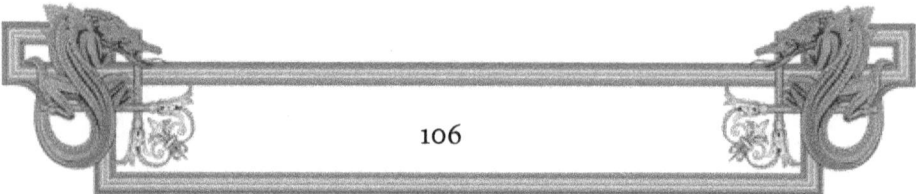

extreme tendencies – by demonstrating how much power they have in their hands, but their instinct itself is unswervingly conservative – and "mediocre" – wherever there is power, they know how to be powerful; but the employment of their power is always in one direction. The honorable term for mediocre is, of course, the word "liberal."[22]

The supreme manifestation of the Will to Power is the ability to impose upon becoming the character of being, and is also connected to Nietzsche's notion of self-overcoming. This he refers to as *Selbstüberwindung*, which is a concept originating in the recognition of the role of sublimation. Sublimation, as the mental mechanism that orders and subdues instinctual drives, is responsible for the attainment of "self-mastery."[23] These concepts will be realized in the ideal *Übermensch*. However, if the Will to Power is insufficient in an individual, he shall not succeed in the process of differentiation and will seek to rejoin the Herd. Individuals with a sound psychic make-up and personal authenticity are endowed with a Will to Power of higher quality and greater vitality. Their will expresses the master morality, in contrast to the slave morality typical of those possessing lesser power (*macht*), although the latter may be endowed with greater physical force (*kraft*), and "this distinction between *kraft* and *macht* is crucial to any understanding of Nietzsche's mature doctrine of power: it represents the philosophical emphasis on the transition from physical force to mental and spiritual power."[24] Through this process of self-sublimation, the actualized *macht* essentially becomes a work of art, another reason why the *Übermensch* is comparable

---

[22] NIETZSCHE, *The Will to Power*, 462.

[23] GOLUMB, J., "Philosophical Anthropology" in *Nietzsche, Godfather of Fascism? On the Uses and Abuses of Philosophy*, eds. GOLOMB, J., & WISTRICH R. S. (Princeton: Princeton University Press, 2002), 20.

[24] Ibid.

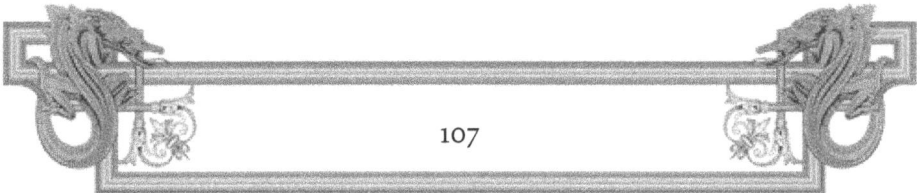

to an artist. The authentic selfhood of the *Übermensch*, like that of "the exceptional Greeks," is achieved by one's ability to bring about a "transfiguration of nature," a purification of the primitive, coarse element of force into refined, creative power.[25]

In Martin Heidegger's analysis of what Nietzsche calls values, there are also conditions that make the Will to Power possible. They do not exist independently, but only as conditions that are useful for the preservation and enhancement of one of the constructs of domination into which Will to Power forms itself: "Values are the conditions with which power as such must reckon [...] Values are in the first place the conditions of enhancement that the Will to Power has in view."[26]

Nietzsche constantly speaks of power being in "itself the 'enhancement of power.'"[27] Will and power, therefore, "are self-same in the metaphysical sense that they cohere in the one original essence of the will to power"; in thinking the "essence" of either will or power, we do not think them alone, but rather, think will to power. Hence, the Will to Power means empowering to the point of excelling. This too is linked to the virtues that Nietzsche lists as being aristocratic:

> The Will to Power appears [...] among the strongest, richest, most independent, most courageous, as "love of mankind," of "the people," of the gospel, of truth, God; as sympathy; "self-sacrifice," etc.; as overpowering, bearing away with oneself, taking into one's service, as instinctive self-involvement with a great quantum of power to which one is able to give direction: the hero, the prophet, the Caesar, the savior, the shepherd.[28]

---

[25] Ibid. 21.

[26] BLITZ, M., "Heidegger's Nietzsche" in *The Political Science Reviewer*, 64.

[27] Ibid., 62.

[28] NIETZSCHE, *The Will to Power*, 407.

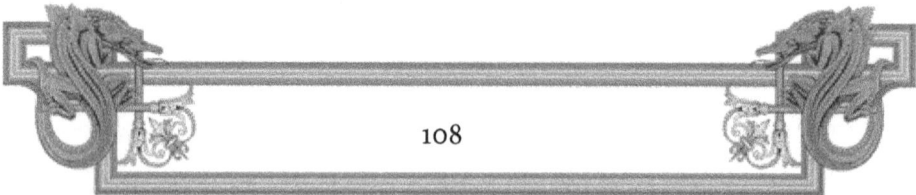

The manifestation of the Will to Power itself it is also linked to the process of differentiation. Like Nietzsche's aristocratic radicalism itself, it is fundamentally individualistic: "it is the power of the individual in will and ability that marks the basis of the principle."[29] In regard to how the Will to Power correlates to the process of individuation, it is not that one opposes society as an individual, but rather that it represents all individuals who posit themselves as being against the collective. The individual instinctively sees himself as equal or above all other individuals; what he gains in this struggle he gains for himself not as a person but as a representative of individuals against the totality.[30] Therefore individualism should be regarded as a subconscious manifestation of the Will to Power, in contrast to the norms of contemporary society, in which one is taught to conform to the law of the average and slave morality. It is from these differentiated individuals that influence is exerted upon society in the wider perspective. This is where Nietzsche's aristocratic radicalism is intended to form the *loci* of the causal power structure. Individualism is followed by the "formation of groups and organs; related tendencies join together and become active as a power; between these centers of power friction, recognition of one another's forces, reciprocation, approaches, regulation, and an exchange of services."[31] Thus, every radical aristocrat maintains the central position within their respective collective as the creative principle until society is eventually presided over by a new aristocracy of creators.

Because of the obvious difficulty in qualifying as part of Nietzsche's aristocracy, the manifestation of the Will to Power in these

---

[29] LANG, B., "Misinterpretation as the Author's Responsibility" in *Nietzsche, Godfather of Fascism? On the Uses and Abuses of Philosophy*, eds. GOLOMB, J., & WISTRICH R. S., 59.

[30] NIETZSCHE, *The Will to Power*, 411.

[31] Ibid., 412.

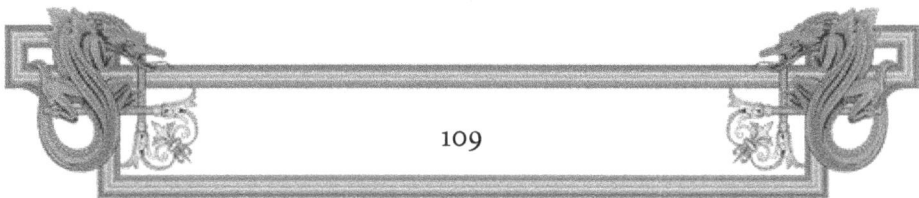

individuals is explicitly identified as a virtue and linked to their capacity for endurance. Adversity strengthens the Will to Power and intensifies it in the correct type, and it is for this reason that Nietzsche relates this idea to his 'disciples':

> Type of my disciples – to those beings who are of any concern to me I wish suffering, desolation, sickness, ill-treatment, indignities – I wish that they should not remain unfamiliar with profound self-contempt, the torture of self-mistrust, the wretchedness of the vanquished: I have no pity for them, because I wish them the only thing that can prove today whether one is worth anything or not – that one endures.[32]

However, not all humans will possess the will required to achieve their goals. Even worse, in particularly deplorable states an extreme weakness of the will can taint an entire civilization with malaise, apathy, and lassitude. To describe this extreme atrophy of the will in a civilization, Nietzsche "uses the term "corruption" (Corruption, *Verfall*, *Verderb*) as a term indicating the general stage of decline in the life cycle."[33] This corruption is an aspect of Nietzsche's concept of *décadence*, for as he writes, "I understand corruption [*Verdorbenheit*], as you will guess, in the sense of *décadence*: it is my contention that all the values in which mankind now sums up its supreme desiderata are *décadence*-values [*décadence-Werthe*]."[34]

According to Nietzsche, this ailment of the will that produces *décadence* is born of *ressentiment*, which has, through the triumph of Christianity in Europe as a result of a slave revolt, sent culture into a state of decline which has being steadily ongoing since ancient times. Through this mounting *ressentiment*, the Will to Power is eroded,

---

[32] Ibid., 481.

[33] SCHOTTEN, C. H., *Nietzsche's Revolution*, 46.

[34] Ibid., 48.

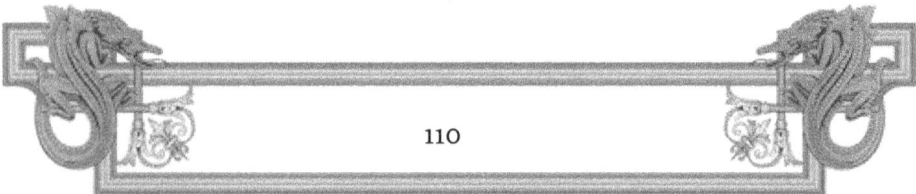

and those who are not strong enough to grasp the power they seek lash out at those who are doing better in life, bringing them down and ensuring that those who possess a greater measure of talent, creativity, intelligence, beauty, or any positive faculty are controlled and reduced to the level of the mass man – or as Nietzsche's favorite pastoral metaphor would have it, the Herd. It is the Herd that aspires to bring down the superior rather than develop noble goals in order to raise themselves up to a similar level:

> While the nobleman lives in trust and openness with himself [...] the man of *ressentiment* is neither upright nor naive nor honest and straightforward with himself. His soul squints.[35]

As such, Nietzsche's antipolitical system of governance, aristocratic radicalism, was devised with his vision of a higher type of humanity in mind.

---

[35] REGINSTER, B., "Nietzsche on Ressentiment and Valuation" in *Philosophy and Phenomenological Research*, vol. 57, no. 2 (1997), 300.

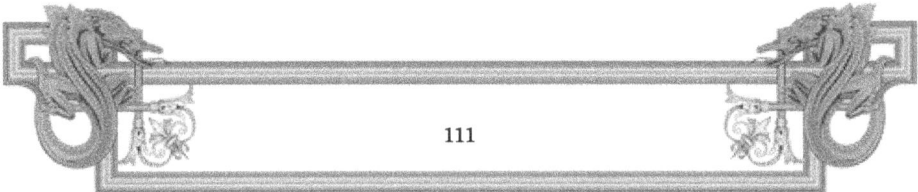

ARISTOCRATIC RADICALISM

A Danish author, Georg Brandes, who was an admirer and correspondent of Friedrich Nietzsche, suggested to him that his political philosophy needed a name, and that a suitable term for this would be *aristocratic radicalism*. Brandes was more than just a correspondent, however. His *An Essay on Aristocratic Radicalism*, published in 1889, was one of the first secondary works on Nietzsche's thought, and is where he first coined the term. He later followed this up with an eponymous anthology of essays on Nietzsche in 1915. When Brandes consulted with Nietzsche about the term, Nietzsche responded:

> The expression aristocratic radicalism, which you employ, is very good. It is, permit me to say, the cleverest thing I have yet read about myself.[1]

Brandes was extremely sympathetic to Nietzsche's ideas regarding politics and culture and began using the term to describe his own political beliefs as well, telling Nietzsche that "I used the expression aristocratic radicalism because it so exactly defines my own political

---

[1] BRANDES, G., *Friedrich Nietzsche* (CreateSpace Independent Publishing Platform, 2014), 28.

convictions."[2] In Brandes' correspondence, he is full of praise for Nietzsche:

> A new and original spirit breathes to me from your books. I do not yet fully understand what I have read; I cannot always see your intention. But I find much that harmonizes with my own ideas and sympathies, the depreciation of the ascetic ideals and the profound disgust with democratic mediocrity, your aristocratic radicalism.[3]

More importantly, Nietzsche endorsed this title as being appropriate to describe his political philosophy. Though various academics have attempted to apply other labels to Nietzsche's political system, this one is the most suitable, not least because Nietzsche concurred. This term highlights the elements inherited from aristocracy, but also the critical discernment that it is *not* traditional aristocracy, as implied by the word *radical*. The radical aspect arises because Nietzsche is drawing ideas from the original Greek context, and not the more commonly known form of aristocracy associated with monarchy and feudalism. Coming from a background in classical philology, Nietzsche was not working with the same idea of aristocracy as we understand it in its modern context. Instead, Nietzsche's assessment is closely aligned with the its ancient Greek conception. Aristocratic radicalism has been examined previously but was assigned various titles, of which one noteworthy attempt is *heroic individualism*, coined by L. P. Thiele. While this is a descriptively apt term, Thiele admits that

> [t]he expression heroic individualism is not to be found in Nietzsche's writings. Indeed, Nietzsche might have considered

---

[2] Ibid., 29.

[3] Letter from Brandes to Nietzsche, Copenhagen, November 26, 1887, quoted in ibid., 27.

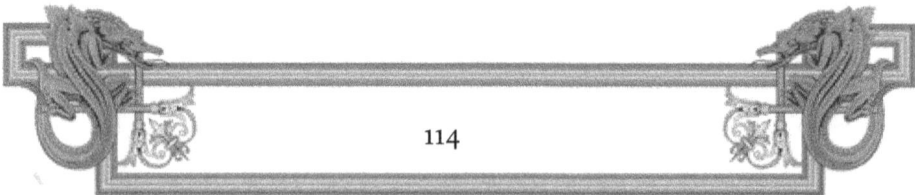

the term pleonastic: in his view, the individual and the hero are one and the same. The primary task of life is held to be the heroic struggle of individuation.[4]

Thiele is also quick to point out that "heroic individualism is not to be equated with what might be called democratic individualism."[5] However, although Thiele correctly identifies the nature of Nietzsche's work as a heroic stance of individual virtue and constant self-improvement, this is nevertheless a significant cosmetic overhaul, which, while rendering some of his ideas more palatable, does not encompass the totality of Nietzsche's perspective as Brandes' term does. Furthermore, since Nietzsche himself approved of it, it seems more appropriate to use regardless of how controversial one finds the elements inherited from Hellenic forms of aristocracy to be.

Initially, the term aristocracy originated from the Greek words ἄριστος (*aristos*, excellent) and κράτος (*kratos*, power): *aristokratia*. It represents a different form of government than that of *demokratia* (democracy). This form of aristocracy, however, is not the same as that of the type of aristocracy which ruled Europe during the Medieval Ages and afterwards via inherited wealth and power. The literal translation of *aristokratia* is 'rule of the exceptional,' in contrast to democracy, which is the 'rule of the people.' Thus there is an element of polarity at work. Even in modern liberal democracies, there is a significant juxtaposition of *demokratia* and *aristokratia* in which a small group of elected officials still hold all the power. Nietzsche's interest in aristocracy goes much further than this, however. Whilst Nietzsche does believe that only a trusted few should be permitted to govern, he thinks this should be done by councils of experts as opposed to today's elected politicians, who

---

[4] THIELE, L. P., *Friedrich Nietzsche and the Politics of the Soul: A Study of Heroic Invidualism* (USA: Princeton University Press, 1990), 3.

[5] Ibid., 43

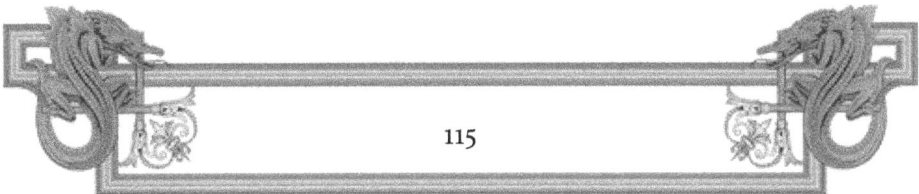

often have no experience whatsoever in the ministerial areas they control. Nietzsche explains how he perceives both aristocracy and democracy in *The Will to Power*:

> Aristocracy represents the belief in an elite humanity and higher caste. Democracy represents the disbelief in great human beings and elite society: "Everyone is equal to everyone else." "At bottom we are one and all self-seeking cattle and mob."[6]

What he is implying is that the fundamental difference betwixt the two is that aristocracy seeks to create a higher, noble type of humanity, while democracy seeks to reduce everyone to their commonest elements, creating a faceless mass where people are devoid of any true individuality. Nietzsche does not perceive democracy as a collective of individuals but rather as a system that strips individuality from its citizens, turning them into automatons of the State. It would be erroneous, however, to assume that Nietzsche is against democracy because it promotes equality. On the contrary, he believes democracy promotes inequality by reducing the value of what is above average and increasing the value of that which is below average.

Other authors have likewise blurred the boundaries between democracy and aristocracy. For example, Thomas Hobbes, in *Leviathan,* describes an aristocracy as a commonwealth in which the representative of the people is an assembly – or, more simply, a government where only a select portion of the general population can represent the public as a whole. Another example where the definition of democracy is not clear is in the United States, which is outwardly a democratic system but is in fact closer to being a plutocracy, where only the extremely wealthy can afford to run for

---

[6] NIETZSCHE, F., *The Will to Power*, ed. KAUFMANN, W. (New York: Vintage Books, 1968), 397.

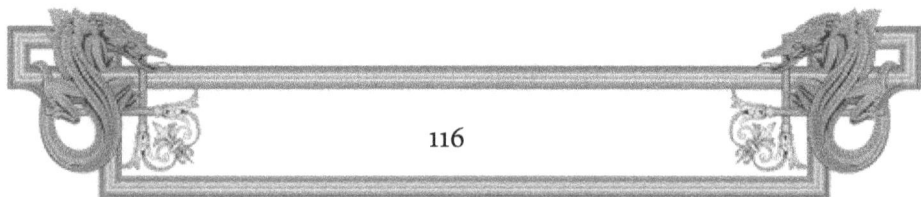

President. Plutocratic influence increases in both democracies and aristocracies when their original cultural values begin to wane. Whether under aristocratic or democratic rule, they both succumb to greed in epochs of intellectual decline. This is also an inevitable consequence of capitalism, where wealth becomes the defining characteristic of social merit.

Nietzsche's form of aristocracy is not based on either wealth or social status inherited by birth. His idea of it is closer to a meritocracy. In order to establish aristocratic radicalism, Nietzsche's primary task was to establish a transition point that shifts the emphasis from the old aristocratic regime towards a meritocratic form of cultural stratification. This would serve to link aristocratic radicalism with the original Greek concept of *aristokratia*. This meritocratic element is what transmutes aristocracy into the new, radical form.

Aristocratic radicalism does not call to maintain the traditional aristocracy. Instead, it intends to establish a new system of aristocracy. As such, it is entirely separate from any other system of political thought and is divorced from all concepts of both Left and Right-wing politics. Furthermore, in aristocratic radicalism the aristocratic principle does not necessarily presuppose either an aristocratic class or a caste society.[7] The difficulty with this, however, is trying to define precisely who would qualify as a member of the elite in Nietzsche's new meritocratic hierarchy. While it is evident that Nietzsche is advocating a hierarchical system, the exact nature of the hierarchy itself is much more difficult to define, for as other writers have noted, individuals to whom Nietzsche ascribes an aristocratic status are of higher value not because of birth, class, ethnicity, or any other tangible indicator. Instead, his judgment is based on personal qualities alone.

[7] HÖRNQVIST, M., *The Few and the Many: Machiavelli, Toqueville and Nietzsche on Authority and Equality*, www.italianacademy.columbia.edu/sites/default/files/papers/Mikael%20Hornqvist.pdf, 11.

Moreover, Nietzsche claims that these individuals are of higher value because they realize higher states of the soul.[8] This is an unusual claim for a philosopher linked to the 'death of God' – however, Nietzsche's philosophy of religion is not strictly atheistic, as was explained previously. Nonetheless, this still makes defining aristocratic radicalism's characteristics more difficult. In light of this problem, one has to accept that Nietzsche is using the terminology of the soul as an abstract concept. Nietzsche often describes greatness of the soul in connection with other personal qualities in *The Will to Power*:

Type: True graciousness, nobility, greatness of soul proceed from abundance; do not give in order to receive – do not try to exalt themselves by being gracious – prodigality as the type of true graciousness, abundance of personality as its presupposition.[9]

The soul, in Nietzsche's terminology, is a metaphorical expression which he uses to attribute benevolent characteristics to the aristocratic type. This is very different from the hierarchical models often mistakenly attributed to him. It is evident that whatever else the term may have meant for either Nietzsche or Brandes, they did not merely equate aristocratic sentiment with dominance by brute force.[10] This intangible aspect of their personality sets them apart from the group collective, or Herd as Nietzsche calls it. He is, therefore, elevating the worth of specific individuals to a higher plane than that of other individuals within the broader social grouping. Nietzsche even goes so far as to state this directly:

---

[8] TOBIAS, N. A., *The Challenge of Aristocratic Radicalism*, 7

[9] NIETZSCHE, *The Will to Power*, 493.

[10] LANG, B., "Misinterpretations as the Author's Responsibility (Nietzsche's Fascism, for Instance)" in *Nietzsche, Godfather of Fascism? On the Uses and Abuses of Philosophy*, eds. GOLOMB, J. & WISTRICH, R. S. (Princeton: Princeton University Press, 2002), 56.

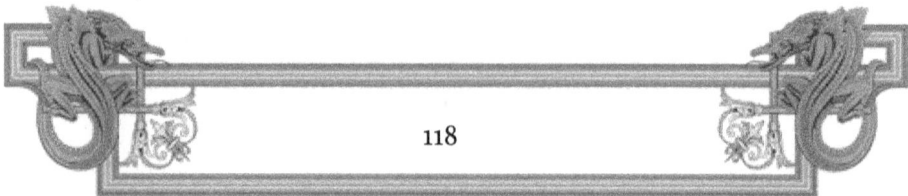

Herd-animals-now culminating as the highest value standard of 'society'; attempt to give them a cosmic, even a metaphysical value. – Against them, I defend aristocracy.[11]

The aristocratic temperament, then, is distinct from that of the collective. As such, there is a strong individualist component. Walter Kaufmann argues that Nietzsche was in fact an existentialist concerned with the creativity of the human spirit and the strengthening of individualism.[12] What Nietzsche strives to create is a culture governed by a new aristocracy founded on personal merit, and guided by powerful creative 'free spirits' who are noble, courageous, exhibit intellectual tolerance, have the ability to accept contradictions, possess self-control, and have adopted an attitude of *amor fati*.[13] Nietzsche is also extremely quick to demonstrate that certain personal flaws should automatically exclude an individual from his aristocracy, and even from the study of philosophy itself:

Hatred for mediocrity is unworthy of a philosopher: it is almost a question mark against his 'right to philosophy.' Precisely because he is an exception, he has to take the rule under his protection; he has to keep the mediocre in good heart.[14]

Further, Nietzsche explicitly states his view on this, allocating a protective role to his exceptional few:

---

[11] NIETZSCHE, *The Will to Power*, 493.

[12] HOLUB, R. C., "The Elisabeth Legend" in *Nietzsche, Godfather of Fascism?*, eds. GOLOMB, J. & WISTRICH, R. S., 219.

[13] GOLUMB, J., "Philosophical Anthropology" in *Nietzsche, Godfather of Fascism?*, eds. GOLOMB, J. & WISTRICH, R. S., 35.

[14] NIETZSCHE, *The Will to Power*, 476.

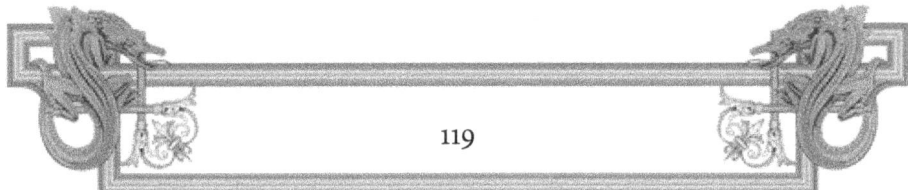

What I fight against: that an exceptional type should make war on the rule – instead of grasping that the continued existence of the rule is the precondition for the value of the exception.[15]

Although Nietzsche expects his new aristocrats to guide the average citizens rather than treat them with contempt, he also states that this type of leader or advisor is never fully part of mainstream society. Instead, Nietzsche expects them to remain separate from the group, in a purely observational role:

Without the *pathos of distance* such as develops from the incarnate differences of classes, from the ruling caste's constant looking out and looking down on subjects and instruments and from its equally constant exercise of obedience and command, it's holding down and holding at a distance, that other, more mysterious pathos could not have developed either, that longing for an ever-increasing widening of distance within the soul itself, the formation of ever higher, rarer, more remote, tenser, more comprehensive states, in short precisely the elevation of the type 'man,' the continual self-overcoming of man.[16]

The pathos of distance is not observed out of the need to create a rift, but instead to facilitate understanding through logic and observation. One cannot adequately observe a group if one identifies as part of it. Nietzsche's aristocrat must remain distinct from the group in order to assist its growth and to accurately gauge the needs of the collective whole. In this regard, from the perspective of an anthropologist, the aristocratic radical is operating in a participant/observer capacity in which, despite being a part of the community, they remain aloof from the group mentality and differentiate themselves from it to fulfill their function as creators/thinkers.

---

[15] Ibid.

[16] TOBIAS, *The Challenge of Aristocratic Radicalism*, 7.

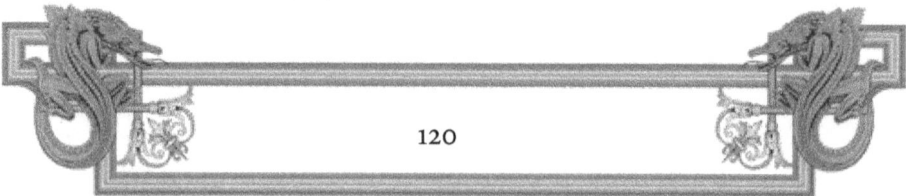

In anthropological terms, this relates to Arnold van Gennep's theories on the liminal. Van Gennep's structure consisted of a pre-liminal phase (separation), a liminal phase (transition), and a post-liminal phase (reincorporation). This was later elaborated further by Victor Turner, who noted that in liminality, the transitional state between two phases, individuals were "betwixt and between" the social construct. In the early stages of development, before the differentiation process has been completed, one who is naturally possessed of the required temperament may feel isolated from group identities; in the later stages of progress, this individual will be able to cross the liminal boundaries into the collective, but approach it from the peripheral margin of the given society. In the context of aristocratic radicalism, the individual will progress from his initial role as a liminal/outsider archetype to a creative part of it in the final stage of development. This role is that of an artist/philosopher who can shape the social model: Nietzsche's *Übermensch*.

The *Übermensch* is an artist/creator or a philosopher of the highest order. Nietzsche uses the term artist here in a different sense; not to describe a painter or a sculptor, but as a metaphor for a creator of civilization. Society is the stone the *Übermensch* chisels, wielding philosophy like a sculptor's hammer. This image of the philosopher as an artist, and his process of creation, is described by Nietzsche as follows:

> The artist-philosopher. Higher concept of art. Whether a man can place himself so far distant from other men that he can form them? Preliminary exercises: (1) he who forms himself, the hermit; (2) the artist hitherto, as a perfection on a small scale, working on material.[17]

---

[17] NIETZSCHE, *The Will to Power*, 419.

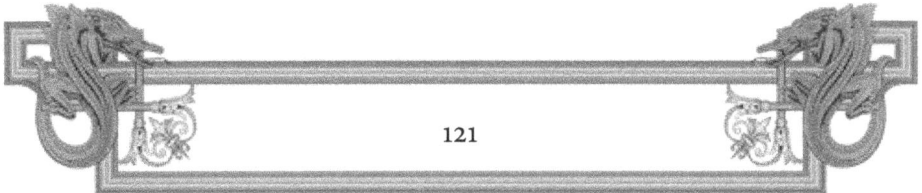

The references here are explicit. One who is an individual (a 'hermit') first crafts himself independently, and them begins to self-replicate on a larger scale. Moreover, the association of the artist with philosophy is a recurrent theme for Nietzsche. According to Thiele, "In 1875 he had already set himself a general task: 'to show how life, philosophy, and art can have a deeper, more congenial relationship to one another.'"[18] These art-philosophers are the future, which is orientated toward "spirits strong and original enough to provide the stimuli for opposite valuations and revalue and invert 'eternal values'; toward forerunners, toward men of the future who in the present tie the knot and constraint that forces the will of millennia upon *new* tracks." Furthermore, these modern aristocratic philosophers will also possess high intelligence, as obviously, to fulfill the relative functions required the higher cognitive faculties must be utilized. In this new status quo, aristocratic radicalism is, in fact, an aristocracy of intellect.[19] This idea is expressed as being

> [c]ontrary to the concept of 'aristocracy' that is orthodox and familiar, the benefit of inclusion among the aristocracy is not that one thereby wields political power, but rather that one thereby counts axiologically. In radical contrast to the status quo, 'aristocratic radicalism' is an aristocracy of moral value. On the other hand, the conjunction is 'radical,' because AR2 [aristocratic radicalism] asserts that, contrary to the concept of 'aristocracy' that is orthodox and familiar, one merits inclusion among the aristocracy not in virtue of the family into which one was born, but rather in virtue of the intellect with which one 'does much.'[20]

---

[18]   THIELE, L. P., *Friedrich Nietzsche and the Politics of the Soul*, 119.

[19]   TOBIAS, *The Challenge of Aristocratic Radicalism*, 6.

[20]   Ibid.

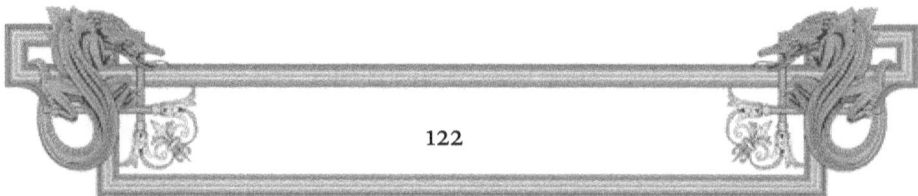

Accordingly, aristocratic radicalism seeks to construct a hierarchy based on morality, creativity, and intelligence. Nietzsche's new aristocracy is not one based on birth, wealth, or even social class. It is a meritocracy of the mind, based on natural ability and personal qualities. What renders this as radical is not only the fact that it redefines the meaning of aristocracy, but that it advocates recognition of the fact that not all people are equal in capability, and that only those who are exceptional should be entitled to occupy a position of power or responsibility. Nietzsche asserts that this "aristocratic society [is] a society which believes in a long scale of orders of rank and differences of worth between man and man."[21] This renders it as a *meritocratic hierarchy*. Aristocratic radicalism is thus not a continuation of the traditional aristocracy for according to Nietzsche, "[a]ristocrats so far, spiritual and temporal, prove nothing against the necessity for a new aristocracy."[22] This presumably indicates that many traditional aristocrats failed to adhere to Nietzsche's standards. Therefore, it is in opposition to the traditional aristocracy that Nietzsche posits "his aristocratic philosopher-legislators at the summit of his ideal social order," and "he defines this 'sovereign authority' as a spiritual oligarchy, referring to its members as 'oligarchs of the spirit.'"[23]

As such, despite Nietzsche's perspectivism and views on the nature of morals, there are ethical requirements for his new aristocracy. The main point of aristocratic radicalism is to shift the emphasis from aristocratic heritage to aristocratic temperament. The result of this is that class nobility as a result of ancestry is eliminated. Instead, it becomes a matter of whether or not one *acts* with nobility – and

---

[21] Ibid., 8.

[22] NIETZSCHE, *The Will to Power*, 500.

[23] DOMBOWSKY, D., *Nietzsche's Machiavellian Politics* (New York: Palgrave Macmillan, 2004), 57.

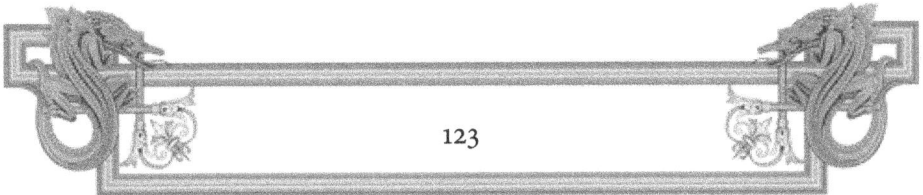

nobility of character is a requirement that Nietzsche dwells upon at length. The reason why such importance is attached to the attribute of nobility is that in the original Greek definition of aristocracy, individual nobility was a preparatory requirement for personal sovereignty; thus it was the case that "[t]he noble class is [that] which inherits this training."[24] However, rather than glorifying this landed gentry, Nietzsche makes the intriguing assertion that "[i]n the beginning, the noble caste was always the barbarian caste: their predominance did not lie mainly in physical strength but in the strength of the soul – they were more whole human beings."[25] This comment relates to the origins of aristocracy and civilization in ancient Greece.

The birth of aristocracy in Greece precedes recorded history, dating back to the composition of the *Iliad* and the *Odyssey* as orally transmitted epics. From these epics it is possible to catch a glimpse of the aristocratic principle in its earliest formative period. The notion of aristocracy arose in Greece at the same time as that of civilization itself. The characteristics found in the heroes of these epics are the same qualities that ancient Greek society deemed to be desirable, such as personal honor and individual strength. These traits were then transcribed into a moral/ethical system that operated as the standard for leadership. The select few individuals who embodied these qualities quickly gained status in this era and came to occupy positions of authority. This period was one of development in Greece, and minimal levels of social order and stratification were in place. Legislation and organization were very much at a rudimentary level. It was a formative stage where the social doctrine was primarily built from the ground up, laying the foundations for the future civilization

---

[24] NIETZSCHE, *The Will to Power*, 406.

[25] DETWILER, B., *Nietzsche and the Politics of Aristocratic Radicalism* (Chicago: University of Chicago Press, 1990), 45.

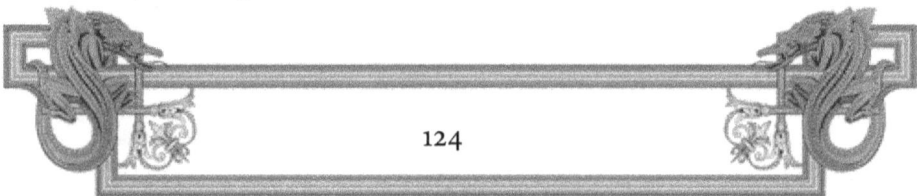

of Hellas[26] to be born. The leaders who rose to power in this epoch did so by their merit, and were the ancestors of the later Greek aristocrats. These first rulers then passed on their abilities to the next generation, in the expectation that their traits would be inherited via the royal bloodline. Even today, the famous euphemism 'blue blood' is associated with having aristocratic ancestry. Aristocrats then married other aristocrats – the bloodline of the kings was firmly cemented, and power passed only into the hands of those who could claim such status by descent.

The first leaders of Greece came to be so because they were skilled in war and combat – not in a brutish sense, but in a heroic one which required social and strategic skills as well as mere physical force. The desirable qualities in this first phase of Greek aristocracy were closely aligned with the Homeric ideal. This ideal required standards of ethics and personal behavior, as illustrated in the epics by the use of terms such as good (*agathos, esthlos*) and bad (*kakos*); these refer almost exclusively to the sphere of physical excellence and bravery, with *agathos* in particular being conferred upon high-status warriors.[27] The concept of *areté* (excellence) is also of great importance in understanding the nature of Hellenic aristocracy. Tyrtaeus provides the following description of *areté* for the Homeric warrior:

> For a man is not *agathos* in war, unless he endure seeing the bloody slaughter, and standing close reach out for the foe. This is *areté*, this is the best and loveliest prize for the young win. A common good this, for the whole *polis* and all the *demos*, when a man holds, firm-set among the fighters, unflinchingly.

---

[26]   Hellas is the original name for Greece.

[27]   DONLAN, W., *The Aristocratic Ideal and Selected Papers* (Wauconda, IL: Bolchazy-Carducci Publishers, 1999), 32.

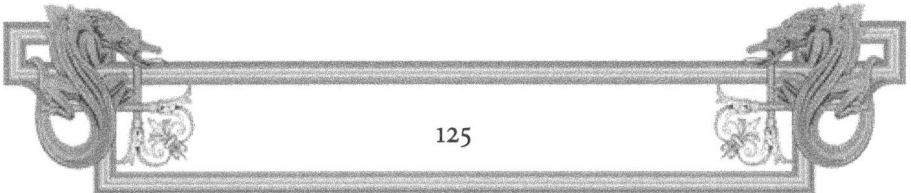

Areté is a highly ambiguous word encompassing both *excellence* and *honor* (*timé*). *Timé* was an essential quality for the warrior ethos in this period, but it began to wane when the tribal kingdoms grew in size to form the *polis*. These two concepts are the key to understanding the aristocratic principle, with *areté* in particular functioning as the vital core of the Hellenic aristocracy. In this early period, *areté* could be conferred by individual merit and having value for society. The first kings were chosen because they were the best of men; their heirs were chosen out of a belief that these good qualities were inherited via the bloodline. Thus, *areté* is the primary character trait associated with the early development of aristocracy, and this arises not from the art-philosophers Nietzsche also extols, but from the warrior nobility of the barbarians, who, through the rule of combat, became the first aristocrats. Nobility of character is what serves to provide a connection between these rugged, heroic barbarians of antiquity with the significantly less macho image of the art-philosopher. The descriptions of what Nietzsche considers to be noble, and thus common to both types, are given in *The Will to Power*:

What is noble?

Endurance of poverty and want, also of sickness.

Avoidance of petty honors and mistrust of all who praise readily; for whoever praises believes he understands what he praises; but to understand – Balzac, that typical man of ambition, has revealed it – *comprende c'est égaler*.

The conviction that one has duties only to one's equals, towards the others one acts as one thinks best: that justice can be hoped for (unfortunately not counted on) only inter pares.

[...]

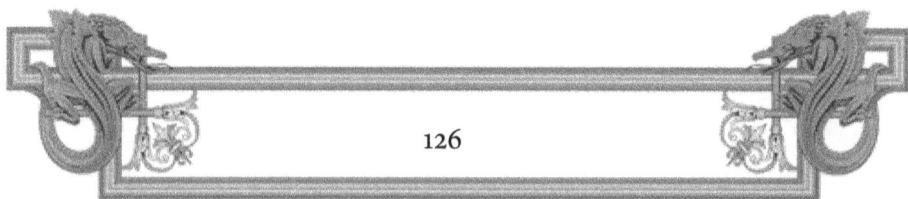

Always to experience oneself as one who bestows honors while there are not many fit to honor one.

[...]

Always disguised: the higher the type, the more a man requires an incognito. If God existed, he would, merely on grounds of decency, be obliged to show himself to the world as only a man.

[...]

Pleasure in forms; taking under protection everything formal, the conviction that politeness is one of the greatest virtues; mistrust for letting oneself go in any way, including all freedom of press and thought, because under them the spirit grows comfortable and doltish and relaxes its limbs.

[...]

Pleasure in princes and priests, because they preserve the belief in differences in human values even in the valuation of the past, at least symbolically and on the whole even actually.

[...]

Disgust for the demagogic, for the "enlightenment," for "being cozy," for plebeian familiarity.[28]

Another recurrent theme in Nietzsche's descriptions of nobility is endurance. For Nietzsche, endurance is undergone in the name of a task or cause even if it may run contrary to the opinions of the majority. To be considered part of Nietzsche's new aristocracy, one's existence must serve a higher purpose, which is achieved by setting

---

[28] NIETZSCHE, *The Will to Power*, 496-498.

oneself "as lofty and noble a goal as you can."[29] Therefore, nobility is analogous with the spirit of self-sacrifice, an interpretation which is very far removed from the average person's understanding of the *Übermensch*. Nietzsche sees the nobility of a person in their independence and capacity to devote themselves to undertaking a responsibility – since an individual, with the self mastery which this implies, necessarily acquires in addition mastery over external circumstances and over other creatures, whose will is not so lasting.[30] This is summarized by Brandes, who writes:

> But be that as it may: owing to our familiarity with the notion of making sacrifices for a whole country, a multitude of people, it appears unreasonable that a man should exist for the sake of a few other men, that it should be his duty to devote his life to them in order thereby to promote culture. But nevertheless, the answer to the question of culture – how the individual human life may acquire its highest value and its greatest significance – must be: By being lived for the benefit of the rarest and most valuable examples of the human race. This will also be the way in which the individual can best impart a value to the life of the greatest number.[31]

Nietzsche's ideas have been appropriated by many people – ranging from politicians to occultists – to enhance their own theories, and as a result he has been linked to a wide assortment of clashing ideologies which have sought to fabricate a link between Nietzsche's ideas and their own. Unfortunately, as a consequence of this Nietzsche's opinions are often distorted in order to support ideas

---

[29]   BRANDES, G., *Friedrich Nietzsche* (New York: The Macmillan Company, 1915), 18.

[30]   Ibid., 30.

[31]   Ibid., 13.

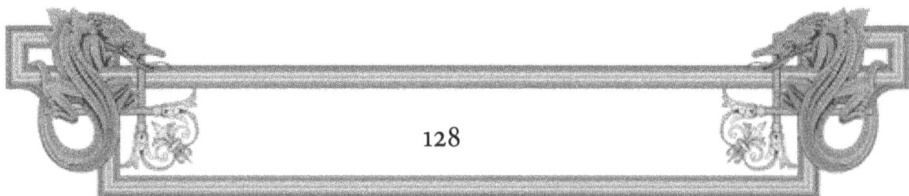

that he was vehemently opposed to. Putting all of these impostors aside, however, it was aristocratic radicalism that Nietzsche intended to replace the status quo, and it is to this end that Nietzsche makes direct and impassioned pleas to his readers to forge a new social construct:

> We to whom the democratic movement is not merely a form assumed by political organization in decay but also a form assumed by man in his decay [...] in the process of becoming mediocre and losing his value, whither must *we* direct our hopes? Towards *new philosophers*, we have no other choice, towards spirits strong and original enough to make a start on antithetical evaluations.[32]

Curiously, Nietzsche recognizes that he will not be the one who enacts these radical alterations. Rather, he anticipates that one of his readers will supersede or even eclipse him. This is plainly stated by Nietzsche's fictional prophet Zarathustra:

> I am a prelude of better players, O my brothers! A precedent! Follow my precedent.[33]

Presumably, Nietzsche's heir apparent would be the disciple who enacted Nietzsche's cultural revival through antipolitical strategies and established their own reign of excellence, not in a literary form but in terms of wielding power in civilization itself. According to Dombowsky Nietzsche imagines this ideal 'new aristocracy' as those who "employ democratic Europe as their most pliant and supple instrument for getting hold of the destinies of the earth."[34] This suggests that although Nietzsche does not see democracy as a true

---

[32] LANG, "Misinterpretations as the Author's Responsibility," 55.

[33] DETWILER, *Nietzsche and the Politics of Aristocratic Radicalism*, 35.

[34] DOMBOWSKY, *Nietzsche's Machiavellian Politics*, 112.

form of meritocracy, he is not above using it as a tool to promote his own goals. Despite Nietzsche's goal ultimately being a socio-political reformation, he is adamant that this cannot be carried out by a politician, for they cannot create ideas in the same fashion that an artist or a philosopher does. This is one of the reasons that Nietzsche scorns such a wide range of political ideologies. What makes Nietzsche's quest for a new cultural framework for civilization is, as Schotten points out, that Nietzsche ultimately believes that this task is a philosophical one:

> While Nietzsche's unequivocal, declarative philosophy – and the urgency of its successful treatment or legislation – may seem particular only to the historical set of conditions he believes existed in late nineteenth-century Europe, Nietzsche nevertheless generalizes this understanding as the definition of philosophical activity. The totalizing character of philosophy is mandated by the formidableness of its creative task; only its successfully hegemonic achievement could render that philosophy "true." What this means, in my view, is that, for Nietzsche, a true philosopher is a successful revolutionary. Real philosophers are the fashioners of the world.[35]

Despite Nietzsche's views on the importance of individuality, he expressed little admiration for liberalism. On the contrary, Nietzsche explicitly links mediocrity to liberalism and democracy, for both are doctrines of the middle. This also relates to his theory of the Will to Power, and it is certainly no coincidence that the majority of his ideas pertaining to aristocratic radicalism are to be found in *The Will to Power*. It is the Will to Power itself which is feared under democratic regimes, as Nietzsche understood: "The will to power is so hated in democratic ages that their entire psychology

---

[35] SCHOTTEN, C. H., *Nietzsche's Revolution: Décadence, Politics, and Sexuality* (New York: Palgrave Macmillan, 2009), 69.

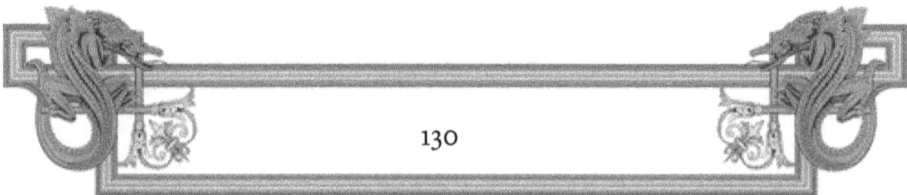

seems directed toward belittling and defaming it."[36] Seen in such a light, it is clear that Nietzsche disavows both the Left and the Right, along with democracy and its entire political system. Nietzsche also made an effort to ensure that his philosophical ideas could not be utilized by them, largely by ensuring that the content surpassed their understanding, as Nietzsche explicitly states here:

> I write in such a way that neither the mob, nor the *populi*, nor the parties of any kind want to read me [...] Neither usefully nor pleasantly to the trio I have named.[37]

Thus, if one isn't interested in what Nietzsche has to say, then the sentiment is quite likely reciprocated. Instead of being tied to mainstream ideas and the Herd mentality, Nietzsche wished to promote his philosophy only to specific types of individuals. As Thiele writes,

> Nietzsche's brand of individualism is neither a political statement of democratic inclination nor an ethical statement of respect for the status of human life and liberty. The individual is not so much a reality as a goal. The heroic task, assumed only by the few, is to become a sovereign individual.[38]

The individual thus becomes a personal sovereign, capable of meritorious conduct and self-governance. Such a person does not require the imposition of any external rules or legislation. Nietzsche is, therefore, more closely aligned with vigorous individuals than with any collectivity or calls for a 'nanny state.' For, as Zarathustra says, "Only there, where the State ceases, does the man who is not

---

[36] NIETZSCHE, *The Will to Power*, 397.

[37] THIELE, *Friedrich Nietzsche and the Politics of the Soul*, 47.

[38] Ibid., 45.

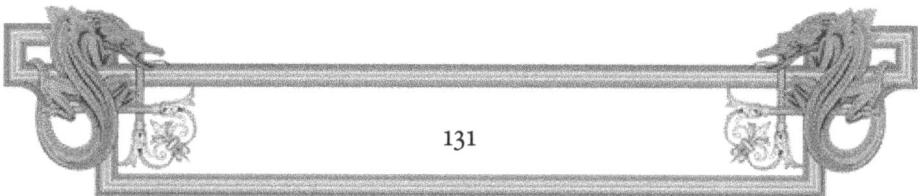

superfluous begin."[39] This type, who is not superfluous, is the free thinker, and such people are the "born, sworn, jealous friends of solitude."[40] These sovereign individuals, despite the distance they maintain from the mainstream, are ultimately destined for leadership roles precisely because their attitude of aloofness renders them capable of independent thinking, which is unswayed by peer pressure and the fashions of polite society. This attitude of aloof nobility also serves to explain Thiele's labeling of Nietzsche's political theory as 'heroic individualism.' It must be emphasized, however, that Nietzsche's ideal form of government is not in any way similar to fascism, monarchy, tyranny, or even traditional aristocracy. As is implied by the term radical, it is a form of governance that is utterly different from any existing political system. Instead, it advocates a government devoid of the rhetoric of politicians and free from the public hysteria incited by the misuse of propaganda. Nietzsche advocates a world ruled by experts in their field, totally devoid of politicians. As Dombowsky notes,

> [i]n contrast to party politics and 'the now dominant belief in numbers,' Nietzsche advocates the formation or election, through a highly selective process, of a 'lawgiving body' made up of 'experts and men of knowledge'; a technocracy, as existed in the Bonapartist regimes. In such a lawgiving body the vote would be left to the lawgivers themselves, 'so that in the strictest sense the law would proceed out of the understanding of those who understand best,' or an aristocracy, as opposed to proceeding from the vote of parties who are, as Nietzsche writes, 'ill-informed and incapable of judgment.'[41]

---

[39] Ibid., 47.

[40] Ibid., 174.

[41] DOMBOWSKY, *Nietzsche's Machiavellian Politics*, 57.

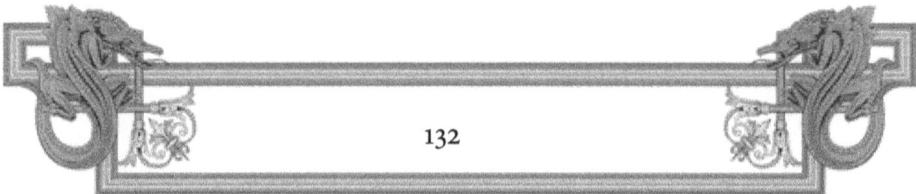

It is in this vein that aristocratic radicalism is aristocratic, for it is based not only on the characteristics of temperament but is also a hierarchy of knowledge. Those who are the best in their fields should rule; not politicians, who for the most part have little or no knowledge of the disciplines that are literally a matter of life or death for the citizens. Politicians instead rely on the advice of their advisors – the experts – to make decisions. To Nietzsche, the politician appears as a useless figurehead, and all the real work is carried out by the experts behind the scenes. It therefore makes sense to remove the figurehead and instead appoint a council of experts who make decisions by discussing and voting amongst each other. Dombowsky describes what this council of experts may resemble, writing that "In *On the Future of Our Educational Institutions*, Nietzsche envisages and anticipates 'serious men, working together in the service of a completely rejuvenated and purified culture'; a 'true, aristocratic culture, founded upon a few carefully chosen minds.'"[42] In such a system, doctors would be in charge of health matters, scientists in charge of environmental issues, economists of financial matters, and so on. The implications of each new proposal would then be discussed and put to a vote – one which would not be based on gallivanting around the country holding social events and mere popularity contests, but on facts and knowledge.

Not only does Nietzsche perceive politics as being an unnecessary burden upon society, he also sees it as running contrary to culture, writing that "[a]ll great cultural epochs are epochs of political decline: that which is great in the cultural sense has been unpolitical, even antipolitical."[43] This infers that culture and politics are not complementary, as many would believe. But Nietzsche does not elaborate further on the question of whether politics is the veritable antithesis of culture. However, we can infer that this opposition

[42] Ibid., 27.

[43] Ibid., 47.

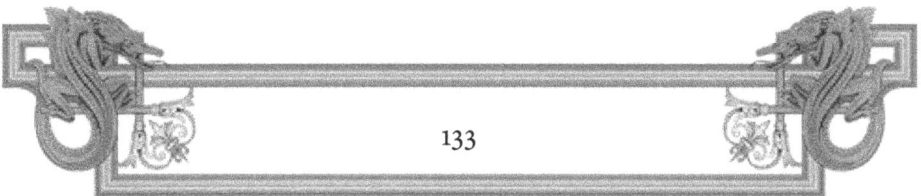

arises because politics is the product of a mass movement, whilst culture is primarily crafted by artistic and creative individuals. As a staunch champion of individualism, it is unsurprising that Nietzsche would prefer culture to politics. Though Nietzsche's council of experts sounds much less radical than one would expect, it is the aristocratic component which is the revolutionary aspect. Aristocratic radicalism does involve the concept of hierarchy, and Nietzsche does not shy away from endorsing its more controversial elements, stating that

> [m]y philosophy aims at an ordering of rank: not at individualistic morality. The ideas of the herd should rule the herd – but not rule beyond.[44]

The ordering of rank, as we have seen, calls for the leadership of experts in a hierarchy of knowledge – which is more meritocratic than aristocratic *per se*. However, this order of rank also entails a call for a new "ruling caste."[45] It is important to note that caste is not related to class, and the two are not even complementary but rather fundamentally different classifications of rank. Class is a financial system which determines the value of an individual based on the amount of money and assets he possesses. Caste is, in fact, a less rigid system, given that it allocates rank according to more personal qualities. Nietzsche describes these castes as being "the preeminently spiritual ones, those who are preeminently strong in muscle and temperament, and those [...] who excel neither in one respect nor in the other, the mediocre ones – the last as the great majority, the first as the elite."[46]

---

[44] Ibid., 44.

[45] DETWILER, B., *Nietzsche and the Politics of Aristocratic Radicalism*, 35.

[46] Ibid., 63.

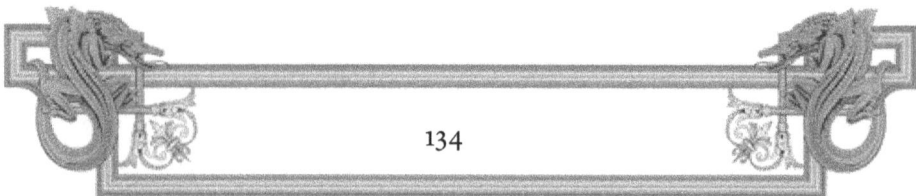

It is unclear whether Nietzsche derives his conception of caste directly from Indian sources or not. Nietzsche, though not fond of any religion, saw the Hindu *Manusmṛiti* (*Laws of Manu*) as a more worthwhile text than the Bible, and although his idea of castes is nowhere near as complex or inflexible as the Indian *varṇa* system, it does appear to draw some inspiration from it. The Hindu *varṇāśrama* does not correlate with Nietzsche's suggestion of types, of which he named three: the intellectuals, the warriors, and the rest of humanity. The first two of these are leadership roles, whilst the third group consists primarily of the average citizens whose role is to support the others. The emphasis on warriors appears incongruous with the notion of a council of experts drawn from the intellectuals. Presumably, the warrior caste is included for their personal attributes and character, since Nietzsche repeatedly makes reference to the nobility of warriors, and even praises the barbarians for having been the first aristocrats. It is also this caste, and not the intellectuals, who possess the inherent faculties of sovereignty and strength, for as Nietzsche writes, "A sovereign and strong will must command, should command because it can."[47] Thus, the two leading castes comprise the aristocratic element in aristocratic radicalism.

Whilst this may appear as too ill-defined to be a serious political strategy, there are other elements in Nietzsche's work which, although outwardly antipolitical, have a direct bearing on political issues. Firstly, as Shapiro reminds us, Nietzsche states that "Europe wants to become one."[48] His vision for the unification of Europe was not, however, the same as that which occurred during the Third Reich. Instead, Nietzsche sees his "ideal 'new aristocracy' of philosopher-legislators and commanders at the end of the process of

---

[47] DOMBOWSKY, *Nietzsche's Machiavellian Politics*, 22.

[48] SHAPIRO, G. & SIEMENS, H., "What Does Nietzsche Mean for Contemporary Politics and Political Thought?" in *The Journal of Nietzsche Studies*, no. 35/36 (Spring/Autumn 2008), 4.

the democratization of Europe, as the inheritors of a future Europe."[49] It is these people who Nietzsche refers to as the 'good Europeans.' The task that Nietzsche has allocated to the 'good Europeans' is an ambitious one, and involves "the cultivation of a new caste that will rule Europe."[50] One therefore has to wonder what Nietzsche would think of today's European Union. However, Nietzsche rejects the concept of the State entirely, so his conjoining of Europe cannot be based on nation-states. Nor does Nietzsche support the old European aristocracy. Instead, "Nietzschean ideology, rooted in psychological identifications, claimed the necessary nonidentity of the ruler and ruled, the necessity of command and obedience; [and] anticipates a war with the European ruling classes who are to be replaced with a radical aristocracy."[51] Aristocratic radicalism is, therefore, at odds with old Europe, but it is not necessarily at war with the new Europe. However, Nietzsche's aristocratic radicalism is a philosophy of aggressive intellectual warfare of which Nietzsche perceives himself as being the herald:

> I bring the war. Not between people and people [...] Not between classes [...] I bring the war that goes through all absurd circumstance of people, class, race, occupation, upbringing, education: a war like that between rise and decline, between will to live and vengefulness against life.[52]

Aristocratic radicalism has no interest in class warfare, racial doctrine, financial circumstances, or even privileged education. Instead, it is unashamedly vitalist and places its emphasis on the

---

[49] DOMBOWSKY, *Nietzsche's Machiavellian Politics*, 112.

[50] Ibid., 112.

[51] Ibid., 34.

[52] SHEIKH, H., "Nietzsche and the Neoconservatives: Fukuyama's Reply to the Last Man" in *The Journal of Nietzsche Studies*, no. 35/36 (Spring/Autumn 2008), 33.

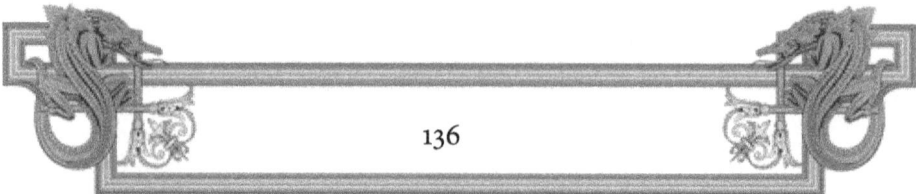

individual's Will to Power, which is likely to be strengthened by adversity rather than by succumbing to it. Therefore, the Will to Power is anticipated to be stronger in persecuted minorities and those who have experienced great difficulties, as opposed to those who are accustomed to comfort. The war is between those who ascend in life and those who do not even try. It is not only linked to the Will to Power, but also to external factors and counter-movements, which Nietzsche believed to be directed at weakening the will. One of these factors, which Nietzsche targets repeatedly, is the influence of Christianity. There is no doubt Nietzsche considers Christianity to be "the counter-principle," or *gegenlehre*, to his aristocratic radicalism. He also believed the socialist ideal represented the "residue of Christianity and Rousseau in the de-Christianized world,"[53] stating that it is "nothing but a clumsy misunderstanding of [the] Christian moral ideal."[54] It is at this point that Nietzsche's more complicated and obscure political ideas begin to emerge, such as the *Geisterkrieg*.

---

[53] BUCCOLA, N., "The Tyranny of the Least and the Dumbest: Nietzsche's Critique of Socialism" in *Quarterly Journal of Ideology*, vol. 31, no, 3 & 4 (2009), 6.

[54] Ibid., 7.

GRAND POLITICS AND THE MIND WAR

he term *Geisterkrieg* is barely mentioned in Nietzsche's work. However, it appears to be the main underlying thematic strategy of his antipolitical writings. As Hugo Halferty Drachon has explained, the *Geisterkrieg* is highly significant, and the implications concerning its use are extraordinarily subtle:

> To get a better sense of what is meant by this term, I think it is fruitful to contrast it with two related concepts: *geistlicher Kampf* (Christian "spiritual Warfare") and *Kulturkampf* (Bismarck's infamous onslaught on the Catholic Church). If 'spiritual warfare' provides the broader intellectual context to Nietzsche's '*Geisterkrieg*,' '*Kulturkampf*,' as I shall argue, gives it its more immediate political aspect. That Nietzsche never uses and indeed specifically avoids these terms, with which he was familiar, is quite telling. *Geisterkrieg* is Nietzsche's own version of a war both Paul and Bismarck fought in, a war he directly engages with and wishes to reorient, or reverse, by staking his own claim in it, most ostensibly by renaming it.[1]

Nietzsche is, therefore, appropriating the meaning of *Geisterkrieg* by conflating the meanings of his religious and political sources. This is not to say that Nietzsche was a supporter of Bismarck; rather, it confirms that he understood how convenient it was to hijack political slogans, transmogrify their meaning, and redeploy them for an entirely different purpose.

On the surface, however, it may appear that by using the term 'spirit,' Nietzsche is drawing us back into a religious conundrum: decrying Christianity, but incongruously affirming the existence of a supernatural 'spirit.' However, as demonstrated in the previous chapters, Nietzsche is not purely atheistic in sentiment, for he makes use of mythological and Hellenic pagan sources. When viewed from that perspective, the contradiction is illusory. The *Geisterkrieg*, then, is a 'war of the spirit' against corrupting forces present in society. Nietzsche describes how this would proceed in *The Gay Science*: "[W]age wars for the sake of thoughts and their consequences; the war in question is about the idea of what type of mankind shall be bred."[2]

The term *Geisterkrieg* also appears in a letter from Nietzsche addressed to Emperor William II in December 1888, where he repeats his claims of 'Why I am a Destiny,' concluding: "[T]he concept of politics has entirely merged into a *Geisterkrieg*, all the images of power have exploded – there will be wars such as have never been seen."[3] The *Geisterkrieg*, then, is far more comprehensive in scope than a mere expression of anti-Christian sentiment. The *Geisterkrieg* is a fully-fledged war of ideologies in which aristocratic radicalism strategically executes counter-maneuvers against Nietzsche's two avowed enemies, : Christianity and the modern democratic political system with which he was contemporaneous. The subliminal impulse of 'slave morality' – which he believes pervades both movements, – acts as an antithesis to his concept of the Will to Power, and consequently, aristocratic radicalism. As such, these arguments also lead to the penultimate goal of the revaluation of all values and the death of God.

---

[2] Ibid., 70.

[3] Ibid., 69.

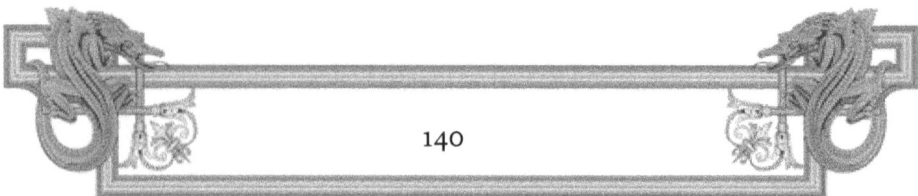

It is thus reasonable to conclude that the *Geisterkrieg* is explicitly a form of intellectual warfare in both an anti-religious and antipolitical context, directed at the perceived enemies of Nietzsche's own philosophy. It is an extension of the ancient ideological battle between Judea and Rome and acts as a philosophical appendix to this history. This war enables Nietzsche to reevaluate centuries of European values, revise the legislation derived from it, and transcend the boundaries of good and evil, all through the lens of Dionysian creativity. This is done to reverse the effects of the first 'slave revolt,' which caused Christianity to flourish and inaugurated a series of effects that significantly altered the entire course of European history.

Moreover, the *Geisterkrieg* is not simply a rejection of this legacy, but represents a complete revision of the religious and political influences which have shaped Western thought over the last two thousand years. While this is both extremely ambitious and unlikely to succeed, the enduring popularity of Nietzsche's books suggests that his philosophical-military campaign has enjoyed some success. Nietzsche's influence over modern thinkers has been more extensive than other recent authors, such as Richard Dawkins. Dawkins, after writing *The Selfish Gene*, primarily devoted himself to attacking Christianity, but never extended his analysis into the further implications of morality, culture, and politics. Dawkins is closer to a purely atheistic and Social Darwinist viewpoint, coupled with a belief in genetic pre-determinism. Nietzsche, on the contrary, often refers to aesthetics, symbolism, metaphors, and mythological content.

The central pivot around which the *Geisterkrieg* rotates is not a war waged through force or strength, but rather a contest between competing ideological, spiritual, and cultural values. It is these elements that are the guiding forces in society, not political ones. This aspect is crucial, for it reinforces Nietzsche's stance as antipolitical

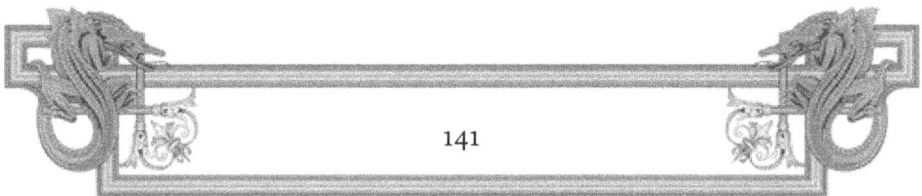

and his opposition to the existing status quo. The *Geisterkrieg*, however, is likewise not merely a literary endeavor, even though the combat is not physical. Understanding it merely as an academic exercise is gravely erroneous. It is also Nietzsche's declaration of intellectual warfare against what he sees as the corrupting elements in society and the State.

The *Geisterkrieg* is a war of ideas that is waged on an intellectual battlefield to control the flow of ideas, culture, and the politics that emerges from them. This is similar to the modern concept of metapolitics but minus the latter's mission of achieving political hegemony, as metapolitics is usually attached to a specific organization, even if the presence of the particular organization is not immediately perceptible. Instead of working through parties or geopolitical agendas, the *Geisterkrieg* instead concentrates on the more subtle attributes of the socio-political process. In his correspondence with Brandes, Nietzsche describes the *Geisterkrieg* as not being a war between nations, races, or classes, but instead between individuals who are either *ascending* or *descending* life. Those who are ascending life are imbued with higher quantities of the Will to Power and the immortal *zoë* that fuels the Dionysian ascent. These individuals eventually join together, setting a precedent for a collective, born from the need to create a faculty capable of producing *real* change, for as Nietzsche tells us:

> Individualism is followed by a development in groups and organs: correlative tendencies joining together and becoming active as a power, between these centers of power, friction, war, awareness of the forces on either side, reciprocity, reapproachment, the regulation of mutual services. Finally: an order of rank.[4]

---

[4] Ibid., 73-74.

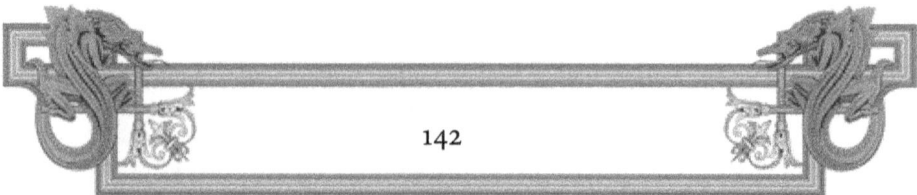

Therefore, rank is filled dependent on the level of individual ability and the subconscious drive of one's Will to Power. Moreover, this order of rank is not just another managerial hierarchy. It is – in Nietzsche's ideal, at least – the ground of an entirely new form for an elite that shall seize control over the world and overthrow the existing political paradigm:

> II. The order of rank followed through into a system of earth-governance: the lords of the earth in the end, a new ruling caste. Emerging from them here and there, entirely an Epicurean god, the *Übermensch*, the transfigurer of existence.[5]

Presumably, this new ruling caste is composed of skilled individuals who then act together to consolidate the power base for aristocratic radicalism. As mentioned earlier, however, this is not entirely a hierarchy, nor is it totalitarian. It cannot be understood as such due to the ruling council of experts that Nietzsche also advocates, who can cooperate in a democratic fashion. The concept of the council of experts and the three castes that Nietzsche saw as composing society also indicate inspiration from Plato.

Like Plato, Nietzsche was in favor of adopting a class system with loose correlations to the Hindu caste system. It is their allotted task: "To prepare a book of law in the style of *Manu* means to give a people the right to become master one day, to become perfect, to aspire to the highest art of life."[6] However, Nietzsche's qualifications for acceptance into his ideal highest class/caste are meritocratic and are not fixed by birth, rank, or privilege. Citing Nietzsche's views on this, Roger Berkowitz writes that:

---

[5] SHEIKH, H., "Nietzsche and the Neoconservatives: Fukuyama's Reply to the Last Man in *The Journal of Nietzsche Studies*, no. 35/36 (Spring/Autumn 2008), 32.

[6] LUISETTI, F., "Nietzsche's Orientalist Biopolitics" in *BioPolitica* (2011), 6.

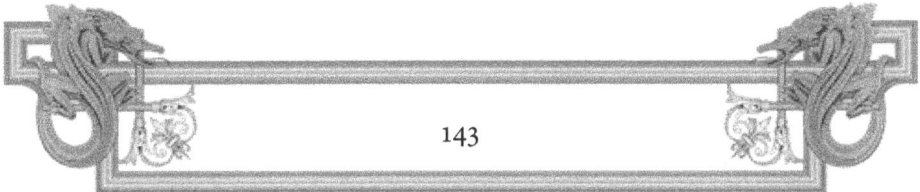

The order of castes rests upon the observation that there are at times either three or four kinds of men in nature. First comes the "highest caste," of whom Nietzsche says: "I name them the fewest." They are the "*geistigsten Menschen.*" Only these "most spiritual men" have the privilege (*Vorrecht,* literally, a prior right) to establish beauty and the good upon the Earth. It is from their ranks that the artists and legislators emerge. The second kind of man is the muscular man – the members of the warrior class. Following Plato, Nietzsche calls these men "the guardians of *Recht.*" They are exemplified, above all, by the king, as both warrior and judge – the executive of the most *Geistig.* The third kind of man includes the mediocrities, encompassing not only the businessmen, handworkers, and farmers, but also the scientists, academics, and the largest part of artists, those who busy themselves with a career.[7]

Nietzsche's castes are therefore not equal in number. Instead, the structure of society is akin to that of a pyramid, with the third caste at its base comprising the vast bulk of humanity. In regard to this, there is no doubt that not only is class/caste self-assigned to an extent, it is also part of Nietzsche's theory regarding the construction of a new aristocracy. The fact that it is to be designated according to each individual's skill, attitude, and behavior is evinced by Nietzsche's statement that "the rights a man arrogates to himself are related to the duties he imposes upon himself, to the tasks to which he feels equal."[8] Furthermore, these new creators are at the apex of the hierarchy, the ones who are to inscribe Nietzsche's values in the future; their prowess represents the physical manifestation of the Will to Power. As Nietzsche states:

---

[7]   BERKOWITZ, R., "Friedrich Nietzsche, the Code of Manu, and the Art of Legislation" in *New Nietzsche Studies,* vol. 6-7 (2005-2006), 8-9.

[8]   NIETZSCHE, F., *The Will to Power,* ed. KAUFMANN, W. (New York: Vintage Books, 1968), 467.

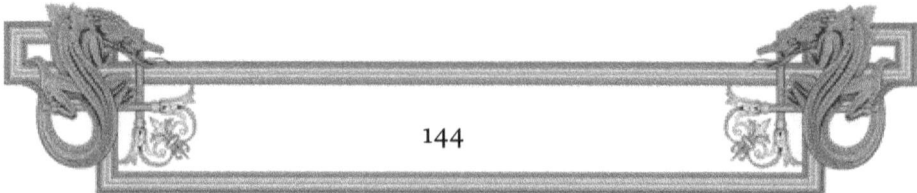

They first determine the whither and for what of man. With a creative hand they reach for the future, and all that is and has been becomes a means for them, an instrument, a hammer. Their "knowing" is creating, their creating is a legislation, their will to truth is – will to power.[9]

Over time this caste will opt to exert their influence, leading to the formation of groups and organizations; presumably, all these will be controlled by influential individuals, between which discord will still arise as a necessary condition of the expression of their subconscious Will to Power. In the beginning, there will be alliances between competing individuals and organizations until such time that they establish an internal hierarchy and the victors, through their struggles, inherit the spoils of war. This conflict serves to remind the reader that, for Nietzsche, warfare, though not physically violent, is still intellectually combative, for as the French poet Arthur Rimbaud once famously wrote, "Spiritual combat is as brutal as the warfare of men." This is equally applicable to Nietzschean philosophy. The Nietzschean artist/philosopher is no wilting wallflower, and does not shy away from conflict. On the contrary, Nietzsche reminds us that the "artist and philosopher [...] strike only a few and should strike all."[10] This statement suggests that they have not yet realized their ability to create cultural changes and extend their reach far outside arts and academia.

To gather additional insight into exactly what Nietzsche intended for the *Geisterkrieg*, we need to return to his correspondence with Georg Brandes. In these letters, Nietzsche describes himself as the

---

[9] BERKOWITZ, "Friedrich Nietzsche, the Code of Manu, and the Art of Legislation," 16.

[10] STRONG, T. B., "Nietzsche and the Political: Tyranny, Tragedy, Cultural Revolution, and Democracy" in *The Journal of Nietzsche Studies*, no. 35/36 (Spring/Autumn 2008), 53.

forerunner of a socio-political system yet to come in which his name will be linked to a crisis of such magnitude that the Earth has never seen before, leading to his 'Revaluation of all Values' – i.e., the success of his *Geisterkrieg*. Nietzsche concludes by declaring that "if we are successful, we will have between our hands the government of the earth – and universal peace."[11] Physical war in the world will therefore cease following the *Geisterkrieg* and the implementation of aristocratic radicalism, because 'petty nationalism' will end. Thus, if the *Geisterkrieg* is the strategy, then aristocratic radicals are Nietzsche's protagonists and politicians are his villains. But one must also ask, what is the end goal? It is to create a new form of politics to replace the existing power structure. As Nietzsche writes in *Ecce Homo*:

> The concept of politics will have then merged entirely into a *Geisterkrieg*, all power structures from the old society will have exploded – they are all based on lies: there will be wars such as the earth has never seen. Starting with me, the earth will know *große politik*.[12]

Große politik (grand or great politics) is another defining point in Nietzsche's political philosophy, and also the one where he is often accused of diverting from his antipolitical plan to partake in the political realm. Again, Nietzsche has appropriated this term from political sloganeering, altered it, and casually inserted it into his work. In the 1870s, the term *große politik*, like *Geisterkrieg*, was also associated with Bismarck's policies.[13] In addition to adopting Bismarck's terminology, Nietzsche also associates *große*

---

[11] HALFERTY DROCHON, "The Time is Coming When We Will Relearn Politics."

[12] Ibid., 65.

[13] DETWILER, B., *Nietzsche and the Politics of Aristocratic Radicalism* (Chicago: University of Chicago Press, 1990), 54.

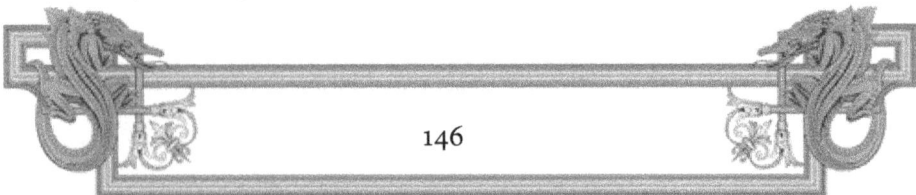

politik with "blood and iron" in *Beyond Good and Evil*.[14] However, this appropriation and adaptation of Bismarck's propaganda is most likely a subtle jibe at Bismarck rather than an endorsement. Although Nietzsche makes use of the phrase *große politik*, "he opposes Bismarck's *große Politik*, in the sense of the imperialist and 'blood and iron' (*Machtpolitik*) policies of the Bismarckian Reich, that 'monster of empire and power, they call "great."'"[15]

Nietzsche's *große Politik* addresses politics from a perspective above that of political parties. It is for this reason that Nietzsche declined to participate in politics at an everyday level, and is why Nietzsche refers to himself as *antipolitische* (antipolitical), which is different from *unpolitisch* (apolitical).[16] Unlike the apolitical stance, which is passive disengagement, the antipolitical advocate is actively opposed to the structure of the political system. Nietzsche also believes that *große politik* is superior to mundane politics because it influences politics by shaping culture and the thoughts of the collective; for Nietzsche, politics becomes 'grand' when it sustains and assists in cultivating human greatness and cultural grandeur.[17] The first reference to *große politik* is found in *Beyond Good and Evil*, where Nietzsche proposes that Europe shall

> [a]cquire a single will – by means of a new caste dominating all Europe, a protracted terrible will of its own which could set its objectives thousands of years ahead – so that the long-drawn-out comedy of its petty states and the divided will of its dynasties and democracies should finally come to an end. The time for petty

---

[14] Ibid., 56.

[15] DOMBOWSKY, D., *Nietzsche's Machiavellian Politics* (New York: Palgrave Macmillan, 2004), 51.

[16] GOLOMB, J., "Nietzsche & Zionism," in *The Journal of the Nietzsche Society*, vol. 7, no. 3 & 4 (Fall 2007 & Winter 2008), 59.

[17] Ibid., 60.

politics is past: the next century will bring with it the struggle for mastery over the whole earth – the compulsion to great politics.[18]

Große Politik is clearly designed to be a 'master theory' disseminated from the top down. In *Ecce Homo*, Nietzsche contrasts it with politics delivered at the level of parties: "this perpetuation of European particularism (*Kleinstaaterei*), of small politics [has] deprived Europe of its meaning, of its reason – [has] driven it into a dead-end street."[19] Not only this, but the entire notion of the State is a concept which Nietzsche challenges, saying that "State I call it where all drink poison, the good and the wicked; State, where all lose themselves, the good and the wicked; State, where the slow suicide of all is called 'life.'"[20] The State, as a bureaucratic and artificial construct representing society, is opposed to the more organic and fluid nature of culture. The State is therefore an undesirable model of legislation and civil control. He believes that it is culture that really forms nations. The State, by contrast, is more likely to be associated with a mass-mentality and a type of individual who Nietzsche refers to as a 'cultural philistine':

> From the State the exceptional individual cannot expect much. He is seldom benefited by being taken into its service; the only certain advantage it can give him is complete independence. Only real culture will prevent him being too early tired out or used up, and will spare him the exhausting struggle against culture-philistinism.[21]

---

[18] HALFERTY DROCHON, "The Time is Coming When We Will Relearn Politics," 71.

[19] SIL, N. P., "Vivekananda and Nietzsche as Critics of Western Bourgeois Civilization" in *Virginia Review of Asian Studies*, no. v (Fall 2003), 9.

[20] Ibid., 9.

[21] BRANDES, G., *Friedrich Nietzsche* (New York: The Macmillan Company, 1915), 13.

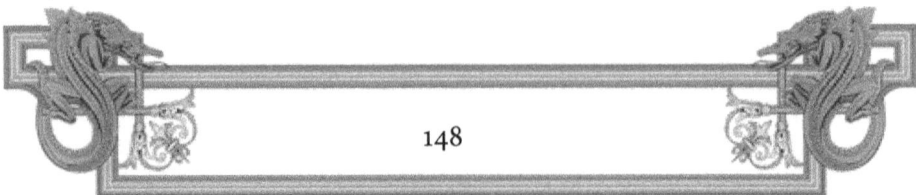

These exceptional individuals are defenders not of the State, but of culture. By contrast, the cultural philistines live for the moment, are oblivious to history, and are devoid of interest in the higher elements of art and society. The term cultural philistine establishes a dichotomy between pop-culture based on arbitrary rule by the State and the social fads derived from them, and the deeper ties which are found in concepts such as *Volksgeist* and the *Zeitgeist*. The cultural philistine is oblivious to true art, history, music, literature, or any form of bond with his own community and mistakes the artificially-produced products of the State for culture. Whatever is visible to the eye is culture, for the cultural philistine. The cultural philistine also mistakes education for culture, and "if he has been told that culture presupposes a homogeneous stamp of mind, he is confirmed in his good opinion of himself, since everywhere he meets with educated people of his own sort, and since schools, universities and academies are adapted to his requirements and fashioned on the model corresponding to his cultivation."[22] Today, it is easy to associate cultural philistines with the qualities exhibited by a consumerist or hyper-capitalist mindset, wherein the language of social media is the norm, Apple products are status symbols, football is culture, and McDonald's represents national cuisine. If anything, the type of person Nietzsche described as the cultural philistine is probably more commonly found in the modern era than it was in his lifetime. Given the predominance of the cultural philistines, who believe that culture stems from the State, corporations, and cultural fads, how is it possible to resurrect an interest in real culture? Nietzsche answers:

> When the men of a community are steadily working for the production of single great men. From this highest aim all the others follow. And what State is farthest removed from a State of culture? That in which men energetically and with united forces resist the appearance of great men, partly by preventing the

---

[22] BRANDES, *Friedrich Nietzsche*, 7.

cultivation of the soil required for the growth of genius, partly by obstinately opposing everything in the shape of genius that appears amongst them. Such a state is more remote from culture than that of sheer barbarism.[23]

Culture can therefore be established if people work together to place greater value upon producing individuals who are capable of creating and shaping the current to produce great works, instead of cultivating a mindset dependent on the autocratic State. Moreover, the State, while it generates an increasing amount of cultural philistines, is throttling and abnegating the Will to Power, producing nothing more than subservience and political values which do nothing to enrich the civilization.

For Nietzsche, only artists and philosophers are capable of launching – and winning – his *Geisterkrieg*. However, due to the prevalence of capitalism and a society centered on mass production, the influence of artists and philosophers has been severely impaired. As a consequence of this, petty nationalism, pathetic party squabbles, and hyperpartisan politics have engulfed the globe, leaving little space free for any form of creativity in the intellectual, artistic, or political realms. Though Nietzsche remains antipolitical in the sense that he believes that the system of governance needs to be completely reformed, the implementation of the *Geisterkrieg* and *große politik* do rely on using Machiavellian political tactics to formulate the end of politics as we currently know it, with the ultimate goal of establishing aristocratic radicalism. As such, the *Geisterkrieg* and *große politik* are a form of politics, but Nietzsche's goal remains antipolitical: an end to all party-based politics, with political parties being replaced by a leading council of experts composed of the two higher castes of aristocratic radicalism. Politics, as it is currently understood, would simply cease to exist.

---

[23] Ibid., 12.

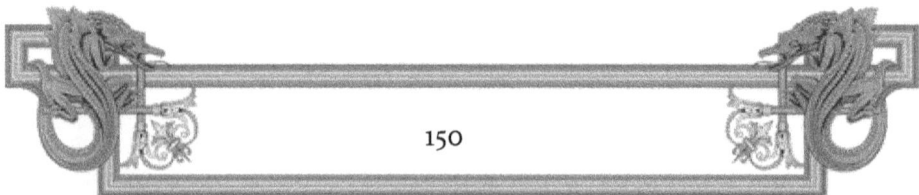

What Nietzsche begins with the *Geisterkrieg* he continues with *große politik*, stating that "the leveling out of European man is the great process which cannot be impeded; it should be speeded up even further."[24] The principle here is the same as that as the second law of thermodynamics, but applied on a social scale: an increase in entropy accounts for the irreversibility of natural processes, and entropy eventually overwhelms the system. The aristocratic radical thus merely waits for Nature to run her course and the political system to collapse from the weight of its inertia. Nietzsche's goal is therefore not to directly attack his opponents, for he perceives their fall to be inevitable. By merely accelerating the 'leveling' their demise can be expedited. In the meantime, Nietzsche perpetuates intellectual conflict through the *Geisterkrieg* and *große politik*. Thus, it is a war of the spirit waged by individuals who, by acting as thinkers, form groups around themselves, eventually formulating their own culture which will shun the old, ineffective political methods. As such, Nietzsche's true aristocratic radical is embodied in one who is ascending life, has a noble temperament, and demonstrates expertise in their chosen field.

---

[24] NIETZSCHE, F., *Nietzsche: Writings from the Late Notebooks*, ed. BITTER, R., trans. STURGE, K. (Cambridge: Cambridge University Press, 2003), 166.

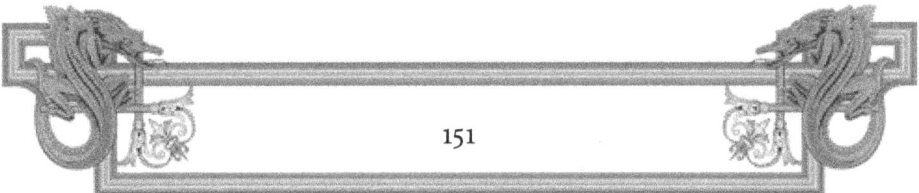

ADDENDUM

CONCLUSION

any readers express difficulty in interpreting Nietzsche's political system correctly because it does not conform to any existing contemporary model, which leads to erroneous interpretations and deliberate falsifications. The inevitable outcome of this process has been that both academics and outsiders alike have politicized an author, who true to his own words, really was not interested in politics at the 'party' level. It is painfully evident that Nietzsche was against socialism, democracy, antisemitism, nationalism, anarchism, and almost everything that revolved around the populist politics of the masses or utilized *ressentiment*. Despite functioning as a critic of contemporary politics and attempting to create a model for the governance of a civilization, Nietzsche remains antipolitical. He does provide a critique of politics, and at times appear to diverge into a political agenda, but at the crux of his theory is a world where politics (as we currently understand the term) does not exist. Nietzsche's ideal world is not ruled by political parties but by councils of experts and logic.

Along similar lines, it does not entail a political Left or Right – only a hierarchy of those who ascend and descend in life. Nietzsche was essentially promoting a hierarchical society based on intelligence, personal qualities, and individual merit. This idea is vaguely similar to Plato's *Republic*. However, Nietzsche does not stipulate that his new aristocracy was to be composed primarily of philosophers. Instead, they are defined as spiritual (in a non-denominational sense), artists, creators, legislators, and warriors. In any regard, it is evident that in his paradigm the creators are at the top of the hierarchy, and there are no political parties.

Nonetheless, *große politik* is expected to maintain a polite distance from what Nietzsche rejects as petty political systems in favor of doctrines capable of spreading and disseminating over the entire Earth. In line with his rejection of nationalism, Nietzsche favors a form of thinking which is not geographically linked to any specific location. *Große politik* was intended by Nietzsche to be a universal political method that could be applied anywhere. It is not a 'one-world government,' but a 'one world theory.' This would empower a new hierarchy that could displace the political values inherited from Christianity when the *revaluation or transvaluation of all values* occurs. This event begins when Europe realizes it is in significant decline and examines its heritage to find the root cause of its waning power. At this point, Europe then denounces the values behind its fall – which, according to Nietzsche, are socialism and Christianity. However, it is imperative to understand that Nietzsche's statements are contextually based within the era in which he lived. Had Nietzsche been alive in our time, he may not have became an avowed enemy of either Christianity or the democratic values of the State which arise from it.

Nietzsche seeks to construct a world where religious power is reduced and replaced by vibrant myths from ancient civilizations. The residents of this world would then reaffirm their identity through the shared experience of culture. In this alternative realm, the effects of Christianity on Western culture are not destroyed but merely abnegated. This is the reason why Nietzsche places enormous emphasis on Apollo and Dionysus – not for their creative roles in the arts – but because they are eternal symbols of the past that are

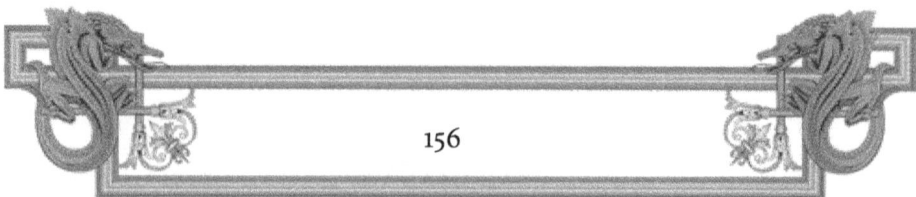

resurrected in a future that has yet to born. For Nietzsche, Dionysus is not just a pagan god, but a symbol of the Will, a primordial power that is eternally reborn, which Nietzsche identifies with the Antichrist. As such, Dionysus represents the volcanic power of the Chthonic forces that erupt violently from the Earth to herald the end of the established order and the beginning of a new eon.

Yet even this is not a complete obliteration. As fundamental principles, religions, spiritual traditions, and cultures can only be replaced and not eliminated. To this end, Nietzsche supplants Jesus with Dionysus and democracy with aristocratic radicalism. Nietzsche's works do not advocate the destruction of concepts, but the creation of substitutes that act as an intellectual and cultural vanguard for ideas that arise independently of the political and religious order. Ultimately, it is a philosophy for sovereign individuals and not those who prefer to be led by others.

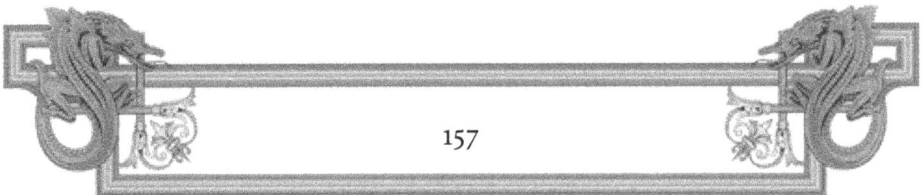

ABOUT THE AUTHOR

Gwendolyn Taunton was born in Queensland (Australia) and raised in Christchurch (New Zealand). She relocated back to Australia following a series of destructive earthquakes in 2010-2011.

 Gwendolyn has an extensive academic background in Philosophy, Hinduism, Buddhism, and Information Technology. In 2009 she won the $10,000 *Ashton Wylie Award for Literary Excellence* for her first book *Primordial Traditions*, which was presented by the Mayor of Auckland. She has previously been employed as a graphic designer and web developer for the University of Canterbury and the Ministry of Research, Science, & Technology.

Her natural habit is a spacious home in rural Australia, filled with books, animals, exotic plants, and religious antiquities. Gwendolyn is strongly pro-environment and is concerned with animal welfare.